THE PREPPER'S SURVIVAL BIBLE

[12 in 1]

A Powerful Guide to Protect Your Loved Ones from Any Worst Scenario | The Best Life-Saving Strategies to Survive Off-Grid Living

JASON SHELTER

TABLE OF CONTENTS

Our civilization is getting more and more unstable, and the mechanisms in which our world operates are becoming less and less sustainable. Our natural resources are being drained quicker than we can conceive due to the planet's expanding population, a desire for a faster-paced lifestyle, technological improvements, and a growing self-centered style of living among many people. Our present predicament suggests that we may eventually need to look for new means of subsistence. Let's assume that the unimaginable occurs, such as a worldwide market meltdown, a natural calamity that has a profound impact on the globe, a famine, or a protracted war. At that point, we'll understand how vital it is to be ready for the unexpected. However, it is useless to wait for such catastrophes to occur. Take immediate action. But you may wonder, "Where do I even begin?" The solution is not complicated; all you need to do is enlighten yourself on what you need to prepare for, the several methods you may prepare, and how. You may then take the necessary action to construct a framework to develop your action plan after knowing more about it. Stockpiling food and water is only one aspect of living a prepared lifestyle. It begins with adopting a new attitude that anticipates events before they happen and acting appropriately to lessen their consequences.

Non-preppers often believe that preppers are overly paranoid individuals. However, nothing could be more false! Preppers are just people who have adopted the mindset of preparing for the future, taking responsibility for taking care of their family and themselves and making the most use of their resources. We can all think of a recent occurrence that illustrates the value of being ready for anything. The Covid19 epidemic struck the globe at the start of 2020. As soon as the news spread that there would be a lockdown, people's hearts sank, and they rushed to the supermarkets in an attempt to get as many provisions as they could. People experienced widespread shortages, which were followed by the worry of contracting a virus and a food shortage.

This opportunistic method of handling a catastrophe was the least effective, and as a result, repercussions emerged. Preppers who were equipped to handle this situation didn't need to worry or rush out to purchase supplies. When problems arise, planning beforehand provides less interruption. Events of this kind really drive home the need for planning.

We are aware that preparation may be a taxing exercise and that the idea of living off the grid might conjure up images of a laborious and difficult endeavor. People are frightened by the concept of packing up everything because they are unsure of what will happen next. Many individuals in a society where the government is responsible for meeting everyone's needs would question if they could exist altogether without being completely reliant on the services that the government provides.

We also recognize that, as a beginner, you, the reader, could feel unprepared for survival in the woods and that the idea of such conditions can be scary. Or maybe you like camping or survivalism and would jump at the opportunity to gain greater independence and escape the pressures of the city. This book strives to provide you the solutions no matter where you are in life. Anyone who is considering exploring the great outdoors should use this book as their primary reference. You'll discover how to establish a sustainable off-grid house and the first stages of living off the grid. Furthermore, you'll get pointers and recommendations on how to safeguard your loved ones in survival circumstances.

Finally, if you have a history of enjoying the outdoors, you'll discover how to live and prosper in the natural environment you value most: nature. This book attempts to instill one critical skill in you—readiness—that will help you with every difficulty you encounter.

First off, this book provides information on the most important survival skills, their definitions, how to acquire them, and examples of circumstances in which they are most useful. It will then instruct you on how to use these similar abilities in both urban settings and wilderness settings. Each step-by-step approach will be laid out in a clear and useful manner. Then, all the potential scenarios for which you would need to prepare, along with the best way to use the knowledge you've gained from this book in them.

This book addresses the fundamentals of survival, including where to look for water in dangerous situations, how to obtain food, and ways to remain warm at night in chilly weather. We'll also go through how to provide first aid and how to look after yourself in both the cities and the wilderness. Finally, it will assist you in learning how to construct shelters for varied situations utilizing a variety of equipment and materials. The most crucial lesson this book will impart is how to adopt a survivor's mentality. Although what you do in dangerous circumstances matters, the attitude you'll require for it forms the basis for all your preparations. The most important life skill you can develop is probably mental preparation. It will help you get beyond numerous bumps in the road and traps. Possessing a can-do attitude enables you to take action and manage circumstances as opposed to allowing them to dominate you.

Chapter 1:

LONG-TERM SURVIVAL OF THE PREPPER

The number of Americans who identify as preppers alone is in the millions. Those who proactively prepare for calamities, such as natural disasters and civil turmoil, are known as preppers. They often buy things like water, food, and necessary health supplies. Even though not everyone is as prepared for calamities as some preppers are, everyone may assemble a survival pack that might come in handy when they are in need.

1.1 WHAT DOES BEING A PREPPER ENTAIL?

A prepper is an individual who has the ability and insight to anticipate situations and make plans for them before they happen. These individuals develop their skills and expertise, gather resources, and create groups that cooperate for the greater benefit. In addition to taking reasonable steps to be ready for the future, preppers often take the time to enjoy the now. A great way to lessen the effect of a catastrophe or crisis on your life is to prepare in advance and identify possible threats and requirements.

People who are prepared are sensible people who understand that transition is an inevitable aspect of life. We are preparing for occurrences like natural disasters, power cuts, and economic challenges that are a component of everyone's lives and are nearly guaranteed to happen. We can rely on ourselves.

Fundamentally, there are three components to preparation:

- Your family's happiness and welfare come first, followed by your protection, security, and health.
- Crises are unavoidable; they often do occur as a result of supply-chain disruptions, floods, hurricanes, blizzards, and other ecological and man-made calamities.
- When a crisis arises, no one will come to your aid.

1.2 WHY IS BEING PREPARED LOGICAL?

When it comes to preparation and striving toward self-sufficiency, there are numerous misunderstandings. The idea of prepping doesn't necessitate that you live like a hermit or deprive yourself of everything that the world and society have to offer. Becoming a prepper or a survivor is nothing like what you see on TV. In the media, people are shown as crazy, anxious, and anxiety-ridden.

However, many people are unaware of the fact that many preppers are quite successful and well-versed in the subject matter at hand. They are sensible and come from a variety of backgrounds, including a wide range of professions, social strata, and economic statuses. In life, they are very aware of anything that may go wrong. Instead of ignoring the warning signals, they decided to act, make a change, and most importantly, remain prepared. Everyone may greatly benefit from preparing for emergencies, regardless of their background, geographic location, gender, age, and political and religious views. It's no surprise that now is the best time to be alive. More than ever before, we are more aware of social injustices. Around the globe, people are working hard to provide equality for people of various backgrounds, races, and religious beliefs. This is on top of the many other advancements in science and technology, entertainment, medicine, and infrastructure that have been made. Even though these advancements make our lives easier, they also make us a lot more reliant on others and less self-sufficient. In the event of a social media outage or downtime, the whole globe is left feeling anxious. When something like this happens, it's mind-boggling how many people feel disoriented, frustrated, and angry. One of the problems is that no matter how reliable a piece of technology may be, it will eventually malfunction or run into technical problems. We often forget that we are the ones in charge of technology and electronics and that they are not essential to our life. Self-reliance is one of the best things you can ever achieve. People often make the mistake of seeking out and creating circumstances that ease life and make us feel more at ease. Most of us are afraid to take chances or explore the unknown because we are afraid of failure. If we know there is an easier alternative, we won't go the extra mile. For example, if you're "too sluggish to get up," you may text or contact family members, even if they live in the same house. If you have a nearby errand to do and don't feel like walking two blocks, you may use your automobile. Life is always evolving.

In the end, it's impossible to guarantee that you'll be working with the same people, in the same circumstances, or even in the same environment for the rest of your career. You need to become used to the discomfort you feel. You must also be able to adjust to new situations and make the most of them quickly and easily. Otherwise, you can't thrive in life or survive the ambiguity that is life itself.

Despite today's technological advancements, we are tricked into believing that it is impossible for us to survive on our own. The edgy technological advances not only make us question our own abilities, but they also make us hesitant to even attempt, which is far worse. In the broad scheme of things, today's technological advancements are nothing more than a stroke of good fortune in the context of history.

Many experts believe that man-made accomplishments have already peaked and that conditions can't become much better than they now are. Another way of saying it; we're all under the impression that whatever we have today will be around for a long time. COVID has shown that the world can flip upside down in a matter of days if nothing else.

Because of the rising number of natural disasters and the bleak outlook for Earth's environment, it seems that things will only get worse from here. In ways we've never imagined, the global economy is shifting. Intensely terrifying. You can see why prepping makes sense when you consider the considerations listed below. There is a slew of real and serious emergencies that might occur. There's a good chance you'll run across one of them at some point in your life.

1.2.1 CHANGING WEATHER PATTERNS AND NATURAL DISASTERS

The state of the environment has suffered greatly as a result of global warming. The effects may be seen in the air we breathe, in the frequency and variety of wildfires, and in the extinction of several species of wild animals. There is no way to predict when natural disasters may strike. Many people are left without food, toilet paper, or even water because of this. There are natural disasters that interrupt the flow of life, leaving those affected feeling bewildered, confused, and in need of help.

Global climate change worsens climatic risks and increases the likelihood of severe weather events. As the temperature of the air and water rises, the sea level rises, storms become more powerful, wind speeds increase, wildfire seasons, droughts get longer and more intense, and heavy rains and floods occur. In the face of overwhelming evidence and severe consequences:

- Disasters caused by global warming have increased threefold in the previous three decades.
- During the period from 2006 to 2016, the pace of global rise in sea level was 2.5 times greater than it had been throughout the majority of the twentieth century.
- Approximately 20 million people are displaced each year due to climate change.
- According to the UN Environment Programme, poor nations would have to fork up $140-300 billion a year by 2030 to deal with the consequences of climate change adaptation and damage management.

1.2.2 RAIN

All hikers and backpackers need to be prepared for rain. Inaccurate weather forecasts led to many hikers and backpackers being stranded on a wet day that was supposed to be pleasant and sunny. If you've got a few wet weather survival essentials on hand, it doesn't have to be a miserable day. Consider the following when deciding what to wear during wet weather in the wilderness:

- Do not expose your skin to cotton in any way.
- A rain hat is essential.
- Choose jackets that are insulated using synthetic materials.
- Analyze your tools.
- Wearables (like super traction and waterproof footwear).
- Ziplock bags, water-resistant casings for your electronics, garbage bags, and flashlights are just a few of the extras you should bring for additional protection.

1.2.3 SUN/ HEAT

In addition to sunburn, dehydration, heat exhaustion, hyponatremia, and heat stroke, extreme heat has its own set of dangers.

1.2.4 TECHNOLOGICAL RISKS

Technology that makes life easier and helps us with everyday duties is also a danger to our health, and we need to be aware of this. Sci-fi movies like The Matrix or The Terminator may immediately enter your thoughts. At first, it may seem unreasonable. People who are investing in these technologies, as well as others, have expressed great and legitimate concerns. We've long feared that technological advancement will eventually lead to some type of apocalypse.

We didn't start dealing with self-aware machines that are a lot more complicated, intelligent, capable, and integrated than we are until recent years' events. A few simple instruments have made it possible for us to alter human embryos. Elon Musk said that AI poses a real threat to human civilization's survival. The ultimate development of AI might wipe out the whole human race, according to Stephen Hawking. Biological evolution would never be able to compete with the rapid development of AI. There has been a steady rise in human biotechnology advancements in recent years. It's possible to save people with Parkinson's and Alzheimer's disease because of CRISPR, a method that enables scientists to alter DNA. As well as allowing for a new kind of warfare, it might also have a significant impact on the world's overall demographics, particularly in terms of ages and populations.

Technology's ascendance means that we shall gradually lose our ability to earn a livelihood. Learning to be self-sufficient is being able to do tasks that previously required the assistance of a professional. With your own food, power, and water, you'll be able to live in a self-sufficient manner. Because we will never be able to match the efficiency of machines, prepping is very crucial. Despite our advantages over non-conscious algorithms, humans will not be able to move beyond their abilities.

1.2.5 DISTRESS AND SEVERE PANIC

With epidemics and pandemics, there are two basic issues. The first issue is clearly the illness itself, and the second issue is the confusion that ensues. A natural disaster, for example, will undoubtedly cause people to get alarmed. With the exception of cases of illness that spread swiftly, this is especially true. People are prone to reacting quickly, which may lead to societal breakdown. Analyze the current state of Ebola in 2014. The vast majority of the virus' victims were African, despite the fact that just 28000 people were affected. People in the United States and other countries foolishly panicked, turned off their internet connections, and even locked their loved ones inside their homes.

At the beginning of the Coronavirus outbreak, people were in a state of fear and terror. As a result of the epidemic, some people are now dealing with OCD, panic attacks, and other anxiety disorders. The global economic crisis occurred when the whole globe was under lockdown. There were numerous companies that stopped operating and went out of business, hundreds (if not millions) of people who were laid off, educational systems that failed, and of course, homeless people who lost their loved ones. Some supermarket shelves were completely empty during the lockout. People couldn't get their hands on anything to meet their most basic needs. This is due to the fact that others were purchasing in excess due to their extreme anxiety. Even with the advancement of vaccines, the number of COVID cases continues to rise around the globe. It doesn't get much easier than this to get a head start on prepping, does it?

In addition, several diseases that we previously believed had vanished permanently are making a comeback due to climate change. The reemergence of anthrax and Spanish flu in 2016 was attributed to the thawing of permafrost soil and ice. Many people have perished as a result of anthrax, which has reemerged in Siberia.

Viruses and bacteria are becoming resistant to antibiotics, as you are surely aware. Antimalarials, antiviruses, and antibiotics won't work on them. In the event that any of these viruses make a comeback, our bodies won't be able to handle the force. In addition to the present outbreak of Coronavirus, no medical advancements will be able to stop these viruses.

1.2.6 BIOLOGICAL WEAPONS

It's rather disturbing that so many countries have biological weapons on hand. Powerful countries have always been rivals, and that's no surprise. If they decide to use these weapons as a final resort, the scenario might be terrible. Weapons that are made from living organisms are often used for one of two reasons. They focus on the economy or on certain groups of people. You may already know that many people believe that the Coronavirus was a biological weapon that was deliberately created.

Foot-and-Mouth Disease (FMD) claimed the lives of at least 10 million cats in the United Kingdom in 2001. An African terrorist has threatened to unleash the same disease on the American agricultural sector, putting it in jeopardy. There are biological weapons programs in North Korea, which is becoming more and more hostile to the United States.

Although they are not currently being used, their existence is still a threat. In 1979, anthrax was accidentally released by a Soviet military testing facility.

That today's technology has made it possible for people to brew up these diseases in their own homes is even more terrifying.

1.2.7 A FEW LONG-TERM OCCURRENCES

In the previous 20 years or thereabouts, there have been several notable occurrences. They were recent enough that you might likely recall a couple of them.

- **Earthquake**

After a devastating 7.0 earthquake struck Haiti in 2010, there were 52 more aftershocks. The official death toll is at over 3 million. A lot fewer people could have perished if it weren't for the fact that the relief operations in and of themselves were a catastrophe. This was an extraordinary humanitarian situation. The air and maritime transportation networks were inoperable. Damaged or destroyed hospitals were everywhere. Much of the nation was without power due to a collapse of the electrical system. The Dominican Republic has a prominent nighttime black patch on satellite photos. The power went out, and no one could get in touch with one another. As if that wasn't bad enough, an aircraft hangar was discovered to be littered with bottled water long after the problem had been resolved. The water's origins, duration, and purpose remain a mystery, as do the reasons for its presence in the face of widespread water scarcity across the nation.

- **Hurricane**

When Hurricane Katrina hit New Orleans in 2005, it caused 125 billion dollars' worth of damage and sank the city under water. One hundred and seventy-five miles per hour was the speed of the wind. The city was inundated when the levees collapsed. In the wake of the storm, many people were compelled to relocate outside of the city, either with their families or to tent towns that had been put up in sports stadiums. Fortunately, current weather monitoring technologies allowed many people to flee the region, resulting in just roughly 2,000 deaths. Many of those folks had to wait a long time before finding a new place to live. Everyone who worked at these firms was suddenly out of a job.

You cannot rely on the system to save you. As of now, the system is already tainted and infected. How can you put your trust in someone who is prepared to inflict death and destruction on the one planet we have for the sake of power and money? It's a never-ending cycle. Other broken things, including the economy and the environment, will not be fixed if the system is broken. You can't help but be concerned about these issues. When things go awry, people tend to believe that systems can respond promptly and logically. On the other hand, this is false. Millions of people would not have died from the Coronavirus if it were the case, and we wouldn't still be suffering now if that were the case.

In the event of a natural catastrophe, dialing 911 is never the best course of action. With so few resources, they can only provide a small amount of assistance, given how dire the situation is. Waiting for someone to help and not acting yourself increases the chances of not succeeding. Preppers are always ready to take the reins and begin again. As they know, it isn't always possible to pick up where they left off; therefore, they are eager to act. They are able to create priceless resources out of thin air. This aids them in enduring even the most trying circumstances.

A person's life will be destroyed if they are displaced because of a flood. They may even give up and accept the situation as it is. On the other hand, a prepper is ready to move to a faraway location and start a new life from the ground up.

Preparation is a huge reward. Spending time in nature allows you to reconnect with yourself and your environment, which is beneficial. Self-sufficiency training teaches you invaluable skills that you may use in a variety of different areas of your life. You'll also discover that you're capable of great things along the process. When you're preparing, your brain is encouraged to think creatively and see things from a new perspective. It may help you improve your problem-solving abilities and boost your self-confidence.

1.3 HOW TO WITHSTAND THE MOST DIFFICULT SITUATIONS?

Even though many tragedies strike harshly, things soon go back to normal. As soon as people leave their houses, they might return to their homes or find other accommodation. Aid stations are available for anyone in need of food and water. In order for people to survive, they must find somewhere to sleep, whether it is in a stadium or a hotel. In the event that everything goes according to plan, this is what will occur.

This is a simple yet critical, ancient rule of thumb to remember. "The Rule of 3" is what it's known as. In the beginning, things go like this:

- You can go three weeks without eating.
- You can last three minutes in water that is really cold or without air.
- Three days without water is not fatal.
- You can live without sufficient shelter for three hours.

This is done with the intention of forcing you to prioritize what you're going to accomplish first. The first step is to constantly create a cozy haven for yourself. Then, search for water. You shouldn't start looking for food until you've taken care of the water. That is among the final things you should be concerned about, believe it or not.

Now, in case you're truly interested, let's discuss each in more depth.

1.3.1 WITHOUT AIR

Basically, if the brain is deprived of oxygen for more than 30 to 180 seconds, you will become unconscious. Your brain cells begin to deteriorate in around 60 seconds. Neurons are more severely damaged, and long-term issues are more probable after 3 minutes. Whether or not the brain is still alive after 10 minutes, irreversible brain injury is almost a certain conclusion. Nearly difficult to survive for 15 minutes. A few of these changes, however, are brought on by cold.

Cold water drowning tragedies may be rescued within 40 minutes, and the victims have recovered without any brain damage. This is because the heart beats more slowly in colder temperatures. Blood flow is redirected toward the lungs, heart, and brain, which are the most in need by the body in response.

1.3.2 WITHOUT SHELTER

How long do you believe you can endure being in a really cold lake before becoming unconscious? Doctors in Minnesota say the answer is just 20-30 minutes, depending on how cold it is. For the sake of illustrating the extremes, I've included this. It seems to be against the rules.

A 70-degree position, on the other hand, will provide you with plenty of time to do your task. In addition to keeping your body temperature up, shelter is crucial because you must be able to do chores like obtaining water and food and receiving help.

Here are some tips for keeping warm and cool:

Inquire about other options for heating in your house. Are you currently using gas or electricity? What would you do if you were without electricity for a long period of time? You're already ahead of the game if you own a fireplace. There is nothing better than having a wood-burning stove setup. For individuals without gas or electric heating, portable electric heaters or portable gas heaters may be a viable option. Consider strategies to improve your home's insulation. The use of plastic window coverings may assist in keeping the heat in during the winter and the cold out. Prior to the development of contemporary insulation, draught stoppers mostly on the floor and the pinning of blankets like drapes in front of doorways or draughty regions were quite popular solutions. Draught stoppers may be made from old socks, newspaper, rice, or any other insulating material you can find, as well as a set of old socks. Your filling should fill the socks, so you'll need to knot the open ends together.

If you don't have a place to stay, a few ropes and a tarp may go a long way. You need to stay dry and clear of the wind while it's freezing outside. Camping tents or improvised tents may accomplish both objectives. Keeping cool is more difficult than keeping it heated. Fans lose their effectiveness when the temperature rises closer to their own core body temperature. If you want to avoid the heat, your only alternatives are to enter the water or seek shelter in a cave with a ceiling of at least a dozen feet high.

1.3.3 WITHOUT WATER

Recent research found that water makes up about 60% of an individual's weight and that dehydration may result from losing as little as 3% of their weight in water.

And when we don't have water, dehydration is what we're most concerned about. Dehydration may occur suddenly. That may make you thirsty and make you feel drowsy and worn out. End-stage renal failure and death are the likely outcomes.

As a result, the typical individual can survive without water for around three days. But the following things will make this somewhat different:

- Age and gender
- Their general wellbeing
- How energetic they are
- Their height and weight, which describe their body type

Remember that replenishing your fluids isn't limited to drinking clean stream water. Many meals are excellent at helping your body rehydrate. Fruits, berries, and vegetables, for example, are wonderful. But avoid eating a lot of salt since it will make you feel drier. Consequently, you shouldn't consume salt water.

1.3.4 WITHOUT FOOD

Despite the fact people tend to worry about food the most, it is really your third most critical concern after shelter and water.

Food may be in plentiful supply or may be in short supply, depending on the situation. If the government's emergency response is effective, you ought to be able to locate a FEMA camp or an NGO that is on the ground and ready to assist people. That's the best-case scenario, but this book isn't about the best circumstances, so we'll explore strategies to feed oneself if grocery shops and the kindness of others aren't an alternative. The issue may not be resolved in a short period of time; thus, some of these ideas are better suited for long-term use rather than short-term use.

Basic choices include these:

- Fishing
- Stealing
- Hunting
- Trapping
- Foraging

Chapter 2:

CRISIS PREPAREDNESS AND SELF-SUFFICIENCY

For those seeking more freedom and independence, off-the-grid living may be a very alluring way of life. These include things like generating your own electricity, collecting and trying to pump your own water, and cultivating your own food. For the most part, people don't follow it. Despite this, many people these days choose independent living and reduce their dependence on fossil fuels. Rather than going completely off the grid, some people still rely on the central systems for things like electricity, gas, and water. There are plenty of benefits of living outside of the city. This lifestyle is permitted in certain countries but not in others. So, in order to assist you in getting started, the following is a self-sufficient living guide.

2.1 WHAT DOES SELF-SUFFICIENT LIVING ENTAIL?

First, let's discuss the definition of self-sufficiency and the primary reasons that lead to living off the grid. To live a self-sufficient life, you must be able to produce and provide for your own everyday needs. Making your own shelter and obtaining your own food, whether from the land you live on or animals you own, are all part of this. To be really self-sufficient, you'll need a plot of land large enough to accommodate your dwelling and any animals you may have. Knowing how to manage your off-grid system and provide for your family and home is an important aspect of the process. Additionally, this may include achieving the necessary mental stability level to face large-scale challenges. You'll be able to take pleasure in the life you've worked so hard to create if you do this.

Finally, you must learn how to escape debt in order to devote all of your energy to preserving your off-grid way of life. Even though you don't need a lot of money to live outside the city, you should set aside some for emergencies and put the rest to good use rather than collecting interest.

2.2 BENEFITS OF LIVING SELF-SUFFICIENTLY

Self-sufficient life has the following advantages:

- **Increased self-reliance**

Living off-grid has several advantages, one of which is learning how to take care of yourself in the event of a social collapse. You'll get a valuable lesson in independence and be able to appreciate the natural world around you. Living outside of society will force you to gather your daily food and meet your own energy needs, teaching you to rely only on yourself in every way.

- **Increasing contact with nature**

Having all the necessary outdoor gear and equipment is a guarantee that you will have a great time outside all year round. Spending more time outside and connecting with nature is the key to living off-grid. If you adopt this way of life, you'll come to see that wildness is the source of all life. You'll almost always find yourself outside, whether foraging for food, keeping an eye on your property, or just relaxing and taking in the scenery.

- **Establishing an eco-friendly lifestyle**

Just by making a move to an off-grid lifestyle, you may have a major environmental effect. Consider how much electricity and fossil-fuel power you'll be saving if you disconnect from the grid completely. Using renewable energy like solar and wind power to meet your everyday needs reduces your carbon footprint, which in turn helps to create a society that is more suited for sustainable growth.

As a result, you learn to invest in long-lasting gear rather than contributing to the wasteful throwaway culture.

- **A more affordable way of living**

You'll save a lot of money in the long term, despite the upfront expenditures of living off-grid. Building a house, installing an electrical system, and purchasing durable equipment and supplies are often the most expensive parts of getting started. When it comes to utility, food, and non-essential expenditures, you'll save a lot of money.

2.3 DRAWBACKS OF LIVING SELF-SUFFICIENTLY

There are both advantages and disadvantages to whatever you undertake. However, it's always a good idea to be on the lookout for any setbacks. There are a few drawbacks to maintaining a self-sufficient lifestyle.

- **Initial costs**

Living off the grid may be one of the cheapest ways to live but getting started may be expensive. To begin, you must consider the expenses of building your own home and any other alternative utility systems that you need. You'll need to save up enough money to buy your own farm and construct a water supply system so that you can wash and drink. You'll also have to spend a lot of money on your first gear purchases, given that you'll need some long-lasting supplies to help you deal with the outside environment. It's going to be a little investment. Regardless of whether you use a solar power system or another method, the cost of electricity will be significant. Since reducing these expenses won't do much good, it's better to choose your early investments carefully.

- **Limitations on roof space**

You may not have enough roof space for the number of solar panels you need to power your home. In fact, one of the most critical determining variables when it comes to meeting your home's electrical needs is the size of the roof you have over your head. Ground-mounted solar panels are an option if your roof isn't big enough to accommodate the number of solar panels you need.

- **Reduced convenience**

When you decide to go off-grid, you'll have to make certain sacrifices. Let's face it, there won't be any U-Bahn trains or lightning-fast internet connections. Pharmacies, grocery stores, and even clothing and equipment suppliers will be limited in their availability to you. As a result, you'll be cut off from a wide range of professional services such as vehicle repairs or building or land management, or plumbing.

- **Uncertain Paybacks**

At the moment, solar power systems may be affordable, with payback periods of 3 to 5 years expected. The payback period for battery systems has just recently been reduced to be shorter than the warranty period, yet they are still a bad investment.

- **Backup electricity generation**

A solar power system must be able to power your home or provide you with three to four days of energy autonomy when you travel off-grid utilizing solar power. In the event of an emergency, you will need a backup generator or battery storage system. Battery backup systems may need frequent maintenance.

- **Property value**

You need to be prepared for a possible decrease in the value of your property or home if you're making the switch to a self-sufficient lifestyle. Some people may be excited by the prospect of purchasing an off-grid home. Nonetheless, many other people might see this as a negative rather than a positive attribute. So, if you're thinking of selling your home in the near future, you'll want to consider making some adjustments.

- **Loneliness**

People you know are likely to live in a congested area. If you're looking for an off-grid community environment, you might not always locate one or be able to live in one. To prepare for such a situation, you must be willing to spend weeks, or perhaps months, without speaking to another human being. If you're serious about maintaining a self-sufficient lifestyle, you should be prepared for periods of time spent alone.

2.4 TIPS FOR A SELF-SUFFICIENT LIFESTYLE

While the last section discussed the challenges of living off the grid, some tried-and-true advice and techniques may make the transition to a self-sufficient lifestyle a little less onerous. Here are a few of our most helpful tidbits:

- Make the most of your new surroundings by adjusting to your new surroundings.
- Frugality and living within your means should be your goal. When you owe other people money and refuse to pay your debts, you can't expect to become self-sufficient.
- Adapt your diet to the season. When it comes to food, you can't depend on grocery stores; therefore, you must eat whatever is in season.
- Wherever your home may be, you should strive to create a homestead. Your personal food and livestock will be raised with the help of this.

2.5 THE BEST LOCATIONS TO LIVE OFF THE GRID

While it may be illegal to live off the grid in certain countries, many other countries and cities provide beautiful and plentiful settings for self-sufficient living. We've put up a concise list of the best places to set up an off-grid home.

- Vieques of Puerto Rico
- Canadian Freedom Park.
- The Tinker's Bubble of England.
- The Lord Howe Island of Australia.
- And Tristan Da Cunha from the UK.
- The Dancing Rabbit folklore of Missouri.

All it takes to live a self-sufficient lifestyle is learning how to provide for yourself without the aid of society or utility services. In other cases, this might mean a complete disconnect from professional resources and services. Many people incorrectly believe that replacing these resources is a challenging undertaking. You'll need to learn a few lifelong lessons in emotional, mental, and physical resilience if you want to take on this challenge, so be prepared.

2.6 SIGNALING FOR ASSISTANCE

Any survival circumstance that necessitates outside assistance might benefit greatly from a variety of efficient means of signaling for aid. From contemporary high-tech electronics to archaic ways and substances that our predecessors might have employed, distress signals may come in a variety of forms.

Amongst the most overlooked and undervalued survival skills is signaling, and it's time we paid attention. The fundamentals of signaling may be summed up as follows: Make a name for oneself by being visible or audible. Using the tactics and equipment we've compiled, you may aid in your rescuing by following this example.

- **Cell Phone**

The smartphone in your pocket may be your key to rescue if you have a signal, so long as you're within range. Where there is service available, your request for assistance is routed to the correct individuals, and a lot of information may be exchanged. Sending a text message may be an option if your phone has a poor signal. SMS messages may be sent with as little as a few milliseconds of access to a nearby cell tower. Spending time in a location without cell service? Consider getting a satellite phone (or renting one), so you can communicate with loved ones no matter where you are on the planet.

- **Whistle**

The simple whistle is an excellent piece of signal equipment for short-range auditory communications. Most people take three blows of a whistle to mean that something is wrong. Whistles with bright colors are easier to find if they're dropped. Choosing whistles with lanyards, rings, or clips can help keep them from being misplaced.

Since kids like creating noise, whistles are an excellent method to keep track of them while they're out and about. If kids get lost from you while out in the open, tell them to whistle three times and remain seated until aid comes.

- **Mirror**

When it comes to non-electronic signaling techniques, a signal mirror is the most far-reaching. In order to attract the attention of passing airplanes, boats, cars, and pedestrians, a signal mirror must be placed at least 10 miles away from the intended target. Then, in an open place, practice with a companion and a mirror with a sighted lens. You may even play a game during your practice time if both of you have mirrors. To ensure that your goal is being realized, you might ask, "Which one can blind another person the most?"

You can use a mirror that has no sighting glass to illuminate the tip of an extended finger and then position the lit finger slightly below your target if you are caught with it. Slowly move the mirror from left to right and from top to bottom. A broad sweep of the beam should catch the eye of your intended audience.

- **Handheld Flares**

Flares may serve as both a signaling tool and a fire starter in the event of an emergency. Duct tape a pole or branch to it, then wave the flare about in the air to extend its range. In order to give yourself more time to get out of the way of the duct tape, merely duct-tape the flare's end.

- **Flare Guns**

Flare guns are a common sight to attract the attention of planes and ground crews searching for missing people on the water. Consider the risk of wildfire in the area before shooting a shot into the sky. When the flares strike the ground, several of them are still alight. Flare guns should never be used in dry brushy environments, desert grasslands, or dry pine woods.

- **Sharpies and Survey Tape**

You may also use survey tape and sharpie markers to send scattered messages in the wild. Flags or trail markers made of electric pink or blue survey tape may be used to direct emergency responders to your location, identify existing trails, and leave messages for them to find.

Incorporating a sharpie marker into the mix will allow you to add clear messages on the survey tape for respondents. If you don't have survey tape, you may use Sharpie markers instead. You may use them to mark almost any dry surface in the area with emergency responder messaging and to place markers on your path as breadcrumbs to help you return to your starting point if you're out adventuring.

- **Adaptive Visual Signals**

Ground-to-air signs, arrows, cairns, and other markers to attract the attention of a rescue team operating on the ground; glow sticks and flashlights; and the finest of all — a signal fire — are just a few examples of the many signs that may be made. In the wild, fire is your safest ally and may be utilized as a signal for aid, with numerous recorded successes dating back to the earliest times of mankind. There is a narrow line between danger and control when it comes to igniting and keeping large flames. There are a few things to keep in mind with signal fires:

- To commence, the fire must be situated in a prominent location, ensuring that both the light and smoke it creates can be seen. Secondly, the fire ought to be in a location where it can't escape your control. Burning a large blaze on a windy day in the midst of the parched grasslands may be dangerous.

- Thirdly, do not allow the fire to grow so large that you are unable to extinguish it using the resources at your disposal.

- And finally, consider contrast. The white smoke you get from burning anything else in the outdoors, unless you've got a ton of fatwood or birch bark, will be the norm. No one will see your white smoke under a white sky if it is gloomy or foggy. Put some brake fluid, motor oil, or other petroleum-based liquid into the fire to generate black smoke that is far more obvious than white or grey smoke.

2.7 NAVIGATION SKILLS

Being able to navigate well is an asset, no matter where you are. If anything were to happen and you needed to leave quickly, you should always have a plan B in place. Imagine yourself in the middle of the woods, unable to tell which way to walk or how to go back home. A compass and map may help, but you can't use them since you don't know how to tell which direction north, south, east, or west really is.

2.7.1 FINDING THE NORTH, SOUTH, EAST, AND WEST?

You must constantly be aware of the location of the north. If you are lost, it will help you determine the direction you are traveling in. By pointing the hour hand of an analog watch toward the sun, you can locate north. 12:00 is where the north is.

2.7.2 HOW TO COMBINE THE USAGE OF A COMPASS WITH A MAP?

You need to be aware of how everything functions while utilizing a map. The first thing to understand regarding maps is how they were created, which refers to how closely your latitude and longitude lines correspond to the real world and if either direction (east/west or north/south) has any distortion.

You can determine where north is by lining up one edge of the map with your current location on the ground and checking to see whether it points in the same direction as the north arrow at

the top of the map. The next thing to understand about maps is their layout. Some will use latitude and longitude as their points of origin, while others may use specific landmarks or man-made structures.

Knowing how they operate before you need them in an emergency circumstance is usually recommended since, if you don't know what you're doing, it might result in life or death.

Chapter 3:

THE BUNKER

Building underground bunkers for survival dates back to the 1950s when the Cold War loomed, and nuclear assaults were a real possibility. It was at this point that people began searching for ways to develop shelters that might withstand the aftermath of a nuclear explosion.

People are becoming more interested in creating underground bunkers as we face the threat of a pandemic. Countries in high-risk areas, such as those along the coast or in tornado alleys, would benefit greatly from the construction of underground bunkers.

To create a bunker, whether you're protecting yourself and your family or just want to live off the grid, we'll go over all the information you need to know in this chapter.

We'll go through the first steps in the process, such as obtaining the necessary permits, selecting an appropriate site, formulating a bunker design, and figuring out how to construct a self-sufficient home.

3.1 Obtaining the Required Permits

Consult your local municipal authorities to learn about the necessary permits and documentation needed to commence construction of an underground shelter. It's important to know whether your area is safe to put an underground septic tank in before you do so. A permit is necessary to follow current rules and regulations, as well as to ensure safety. It's possible to face hefty fines if you don't adhere to the local rules on an already pricey bunker.

To ensure a smooth permit application process, bring all required documentation with you when visiting your local city hall. Bunker plans and blueprints are required for success. Include a map of the exact spot where your underground shelter will be placed. Depending on the terrain and weather, different types of permissions might be needed. A grading permit, a construction permit, a discretionary permit, a plumbing permit, and an electrical permit are examples of permits.

If the excavating and filling of the ground results in significant changes to the land's features and surface, you will need a grading permit. First, the area must be tested to see whether it is environmentally sensitive. This means that the area needs to be protected because it serves as a natural home for certain creatures, has a unique landscape, or has historical significance. You must ensure that you won't alter the land's topography if you decide to build your bunker in one of these areas.

Any structure above or below the earth requires a construction permit. This permit ensures that your construction process is carried out in accordance with local laws and regulations, therefore ensuring the structural safety of your project. The discretionary permit is another permit comparable to the grading permit. If the surrounding area is impacted by the bunker's proximity or design, this kind of permit is needed. In order to keep your bunker clean, you'll need a water supply facility that has piping that goes under the surface. In order to ensure the safety of your waste disposal, you will need a plumbing permit. It's the same with the electrical permit, presuming that you'll need to set up electrical equipment in your bunker and wire it properly and safely. Additionally, it's important to know whether your chosen area is near any major utility lines so you don't damage them when excavating a bunker site.

It's time to choose the perfect spot for your bunker now that you've obtained the necessary permits. For a subterranean bunker, the site must be safe enough to withstand floods and fires; therefore, you should steer clear of areas that are vulnerable. It's also a bad idea to build a bunker in a thickly forested area. It may be difficult and time-consuming to remove a large network of roots. Also, it is quite likely that your permit does not cover an area where you will be removing trees. Of course, you should avoid digging in areas with subterranean utility lines.

3.2 MATERIALS TO USE WHILE CONSTRUCTING YOUR BUNKER

It's important to ensure that the bunker should be composed of a sturdy material that will not disintegrate beneath the weight of the earth. Whenever it comes to subterranean construction, not all construction materials are created equal. These are the most frequently used construction materials:

- **Metal Sheeting** - Durable and waterproof, but it is also costly, particularly if insulation is included.

- **Bricks** – In addition to being very waterproof, bricks are one of the strongest and most cost-effective construction materials available. They may also brighten up a dull setting with a splash of color and design.

- **Concrete** – Reinforced concrete can bear heavy weights while being relatively inexpensive. Concreting that can heal itself over time is a sophisticated building material that minimizes maintenance costs and has a 200-year life expectancy.

- **Wood** - No wood please! Since it's very susceptible to weathering, decay, and infestation, making it a poor choice. Use wood sparingly within your bunker, and always maintain it free of dust and grime.

- Space-saving and budget-friendly are two advantages of using **shipping containers** as bunkers. However, you won't have as much control over the design. It would be necessary to reinforce shipping containers because they aren't built to be buried.

- **PVC** is a wonderful choice for waterproofing and reinforcing your bunker. This material is mostly used for underwater structures such as tunnels and pools, making it an excellent choice for your underground bunker. Easy to install and long-lasting, PVC is a good choice.

In order to build your bunker, you'll need to determine how to excavate the earth.

3.3 HOW TO EXCAVATE A BUNKER HOLE

An ordinary shovel isn't going to be enough to complete the work at hand unless you have unlimited time. Excavation equipment that can dig quickly while still being able to fit into tight spaces is essential. As a result of the need for precision and speed, trenchers and excavators are essential.

With a trencher, you may cut through the pavement, shovel trenches for electric lines, and shovel snow, among other tasks. A trencher may assist you in delineating the region where you wish to build your bunker while digging for it.

There are numerous applications for earthmoving excavators, from trench excavation to mining activities. Excavators come in a variety of shapes and sizes, making it possible for you to choose the right machine for the job.

You'll begin by taking measurements and establishing a dig perimeter. Use a trencher to draw a path. An excavator may then be used to excavate the remainder of your bunker's hole.

Because of the digging machine's linear motion, employing an excavator would result in a more exact and effective excavation. Excavating in tight quarters, including a backyard, is easier with a tiny excavator, which can maneuver through tight places.

3.4 HOW TO MAKE A LIVING IN YOUR BUNKER?

There is more to it than just burying a metal container and calling it a day. Your family's long-term survival depends on the subterranean bunker. There are a few necessities you must remember to mention:

- **Air Filters and ventilation**

These devices filter the air and allow for ventilation, bringing clean air inside your bunker. Your best choice for shielding your bunker from air pollutants and delivering clean air is to use an N.B.C. filter, which stands for nuclear, biological, and chemical filters.

- **Generator**

Your bunker will be powered by this. Calculate your power requirements by adding up all of the devices that use energy. Consider installing a solar engine system to lessen the need for fuel storage. You might even have a backup for it on hand.

- **Water Filters**

Water filters will ensure that there is always access to safe drinking water. The greatest solution for an underground shelter is a UV water filter. Different UV light frequencies are effective at killing viruses and bacteria.

- **System for Disposal of Waste**

There are health consequences to mismanaging garbage. You have a few choices when it comes to building a subterranean bunker:

- You can make it simple by creating a space with a trench, similar to an outhouse. Even if it's fast and easy, it's not always the cleanest option.
- PVC pipe and a few minutes of your time are all you need to construct a simple "poop tube" for disposing of waste. However, they're not recommended for extended usage.
- Composting toilets don't use water; instead, they turn waste into fertilizer, which is great if you possess plants, but they may be expensive and unpleasant when used in confined spaces.
- Many people decide to construct a lift system and sewage pump as a means of managing their trash. Pumping garbage from low to higher altitudes is done by these systems.

Furthermore, make sure you have enough canned food, water bottles, and personal items. Don't skimp on either of them; they'll keep your home and its occupants safe.

- **Make a Stockpile of Supplies**

However, you must ensure that the food is nutritious and shelf stable. Non-perishable food, such as canned or dry, should be readily accessible. Your food supply must be regularly replenished and replaced, so you don't have to consume bad food in the event of an emergency.

First aid supplies, including antibiotics, painkillers, and anti-infectives, should also be kept in your bunker in case of an emergency, as well as bandages and sterilized gauze. Consider adding entertainment sources of any kind, as well. It may seem little, but if you're stranded in a subterranean cavern all day with nothing to do, it may quickly become quite stressful and claustrophobic. Include things like board games, cards, and novels in the mix.

3.5 PERSONAL HYGIENE AND SANITIZATION

Off-grid living is not for the faint of heart, especially if you have no experience with keeping your surroundings clean. It may be the difference between life and death in very self-sufficient living environments. You'll face a variety of difficulties while you're living on your own. There are some that you can anticipate and others that you won't until you run into them. You and the environment around you may have a significant impact on your health if you aren't careful. It's easy to put yourself in danger of serious illness when you're unaware of how clean your environment is on the whole. Because of this, we'll go over the fundamentals of surviving sanitation and how they relate to an off-grid lifestyle in this section.

Whether you're preparing to live off-grid or already have, this guide will teach you how to stay healthy by following the best hygiene and sanitation practices.

3.5.1 PERSONAL CLEANLINESS

When it comes to personal hygiene, as long as you have enough water, it is always possible. It's not as convenient as getting in the shower, but it's possible to clean yourself with the water that's been stored. If you live near a river or pond, it would be ideal if you could take your baths there but remember to use biodegradable soaps to prevent contaminating the natural water supply. You may always use camp showers to remain clean and maintain your hygiene if you don't have access to a clean water source nearby. A nice idea is to use solar showers. Once you get the tank filled with water, hang it from a tree limb, and leave it there to warm up, then it's ready to use. Then all you have to do is open the nozzle and take a refreshing shower. Despite this, the most important thing is to clean your dishes thoroughly and remove any bacteria or germs that may be present. The electric dishwashing machine comes in useful here since we take these devices for granted, and it really helps sanitize eating utensils. However, if you're living off the grid, you'll need to heat the water you use to clean your dishes. Don't forget to thoroughly rinse the dishes after you've used soap and a little bleach solution. If you live with a large group of people, this step is very vital for sanitizing eating utensils.

3.5.2 BATHROOM PREPARATION

If you don't have a functional septic system or plumbing while living off the grid, going to the bathroom may be dangerous. Due to hygienic reasons, your or your family's waste must be properly disposed of. But don't be alarmed. If you're not fortunate enough to have functioning plumbing, there are a few more solutions you may use. Building a pit bathroom behind your house is one of the most hygienic solutions available to you. You should have plenty of sawdust available if you decide to go this route since you will need it to cover up the feces when you're done. Another great way to keep the pit clean and hygienic is to use lime. Every time you use the pit, be sure to sprinkle some lime juice on top. Off-grid homes may have toilets that do not have running water. If you fall into this category, you are permitted to use the restroom so long as you have access to enough water to flush the waste every time. Toilet paper use should also be considered. Toilet paper rolls are usually a good idea to have on hand. If you run out of them, you'll need to look for a replacement. It doesn't matter what kind of paper you use, as long as you get the job done. Make sure to avoid poison ivy while using leaves. As well as washing your hands, you and everyone who lives with you should do so. Alcohol-based sanitary wipes or hand sanitizers are the best way to keep your hands clean if you don't have flowing water.

Don't urinate in a body of water since it contaminates the water. On a rock away from water, where it will evaporate fast, is preferable. Be careful not to pee into the wind or upwards. Predators are drawn to the food you prepare, but your restroom habits might also bring in unwanted wildlife. Animals might be drawn to your campsite by the smell of feces, resulting in water contamination. You may bury your feces by digging a hole 6-8 inches deep and then covering it with soil and debris. After using the restroom, you'll need to wash your hands. You should resist the temptation to pick up fresh leaves from live trees if possible if you don't have a preferred cleaning method (such as fabric or cloth). While they may seem to be the best alternative due to their softness and flexibility, it is possible that they are toxic plants. Pick non-poisonous moss, leaves, or grasses instead. It's better to go for a smooth, clean rock, though, rather than a rough one.

Chapter 4:

GET YOUR FAMILY READY FOR A CRISIS

Nobody wants to consider how calamities can affect our neighborhoods. But regardless of the kind of disaster—hurricanes, wildfires, tornadoes, etc.—thinking about the preparation for disasters is precisely what we need to do. Making the necessary preparations may truly save lives.

Families and children may get ready together. Disasters may be frightening, but being prepared might help you feel less fearful.

4.1 KNOW YOUR ESCAPE ROUTE

Is everyone in the home familiar with the evacuation route? At least twice a year, go through emergency evacuation and fire exercises. Consider just being able to bring one bag or pack one carload.

Which would you bring? Pre-agree on this and adjust if your home situation changes.

- **Create an emergency communication strategy**

Who will serve as the authorized person to provide crucial information? If you have kids, who will take care of them if you can't be reached? How will you convey that knowledge?

- **Delegate responsibility**

Who, for instance, is /responsible for the household pet? What about significant papers? In the event that someone given a task is absent, how would your emergency plan change?

- **Construct a special needs strategy**

It's particularly crucial to have an established strategy if you or a person in your home has specific requirements, such as a handicap in your supply kit, including details about any requirements, prescriptions, backup equipment, etc. Many neighborhood emergency services keep a registration so you may specify the kind of assistance you'd want in an emergency.

- **Display emergency contact information in a visible location**

Make certain that everyone is aware of how to contact friends and family in the event of a crisis. To reduce the number of calls you need to make, think about establishing a specified contact who can assist in telling the other people on your list.

- **Plan a meeting place and be aware of your escape routes**

Where would your family assemble if a crisis happens while you are away from home and the phones are out? Never ignore any warnings issued by emergency response personnel. Roads or structures that have been judged dangerous should not be attempted to enter.

- **Be stress-ready**

Stress is unavoidable both during and after a crisis. It's inevitable, but the more ready you are, the perfectly equipped you'll be to manage it. A further step in enhancing your ability to manage stress is to practice coping mechanisms in everyday life.

4.2 HAVE AN ACCURATE MAP

There's no need for maps to be pricey. In all, why pay for maps when you can print your own at home? Make sure you've got maps of the surrounding area in high quality, as well as any potential destinations if you choose to flee the area. If at all possible, have road and topographic maps printed. Ensure that your evacuation route is well marked on a map, and begin teaching your children the basics of map reading.

4.3 PREPARATION FOR ROUTINE EMERGENCIES

In most cases, an emergency is a sudden incident that happens when you least expect it. If your child gets hurt while out on a walk, in a vehicle, in a truck, or on a boat, they need to know what to do if you can't be there to help them.

- As parents, it's our job to teach our children how to respond quickly in the event of a burglary, a power cut, or a home fire without an adult there.

- For example, if you're confronted with an intruder in your home, the first thing you should do is get out of harm's way and get to safety as quickly as possible.

- Your children need to know how to respond in the event of a crisis when they are at school or at home without your direct supervision.

- Give your child concrete examples of when it's okay to call for help from emergency professionals while explaining 9-1-1 to them. Educate your children about the need to dial 9-1-1 from any phone, regardless of whether it is "in service."

- If someone in the family has a health problem that might lead them to faint or become disoriented abruptly, children need to be taught the behaviors that signal a concern.

- When it's time to call 9-1-1, they should know what they are able to help with and when they can do that. Put yourself and your young children through as many of these scenarios as you can.

- When a crisis arises, teach youngsters how to phone 9-1-1 and include their name, the nature of the problem, and their location. Make certain that your children have a list of people they may call in the case of a crisis that does not need phoning 9-1-1.

4.4 DISCUSSION WITH YOUR FAMILY

"The more prepared you are, the less afraid you will be." This is true for both children and adults. When discussing catastrophes with children, it's critical to do it in a way that educates rather than frightens them. You have to strike a delicate balance between informing them of the facts and the possible consequences of a tragedy and providing them with the tools they need to be safe. As a family, it's reassuring to be honest about what you're doing to prepare ahead of time. As much as possible, include your children in emergency preparedness activities, such as putting together the pack.

How to have a meaningful conversation with your family:

- To practice disaster preparedness with a youngster, just break the topic down into manageable chunks. Consider his attention span while having quick, focused interactions.

- Be prepared to go into great depth and respond to any inquiries he may have. A length of rope may be used to demonstrate knot tying and other skills.

- If equipment is utilized, make sure the lesson is conducted in a secure area, such as the basement, so he can practice using it.

- Perform contingency measures like evacuation routes and explain what may happen while making it seem like an adventure at the same time. In real-world situations, even a 3-year-old can pick up on these techniques and be helpful.

4.5 GET YOUR KIDS READY FOR ANY CALAMITY

Ensure that they have faith in their ability to handle emergencies, disasters, and even an SHTF event.

- Their full name, telephone number, and address must be provided. Also, the details of their parents must be included. Name and contact information for at least one more immediate family member, in addition to one family member or reliable friend outside the area.

- One option for bandaging an injured arm is to use something like an old shirt, small blanket, or handkerchief.

- What do both school and home first aid kits look like, and where can you get your hands on some?

- How to put out little fires, such as those caused by grease, chemicals, and other substances, as well as how to operate a fire extinguisher (age-appropriate). Moving away from danger and informing an adult should be the primary goals for children under the age of eight.

- There are several methods to request help (using a whistle or bright clothing).

- How to make use of the first-aid kit's contents, if any are required (age-appropriate).

- The "Check-in" technique should be implemented during normal business hours. Eventually, your child will be able to text you from a friend's house or from a public Wi-Fi hotspot if they are ready for it.

- Whether your child is having fun in the backyard, on the street, or at a relative's apartment, plan for them to "check in" through text or in person when they return from their adventure. Even for older children who are in a safe area and are being fed every 4–6 hours, it may be between 30–90 minutes.

- As soon as they are old enough to get cellular service, you should have them practice calling you and other responsible adults so that you may be sure they can do so if necessary.

- Children should notify you in advance if they plan to relocate. This means that before they leave Bobby's house to go to Jake's house to play, they must contact you and get your OK.

It's imperative that you know exactly where the kids are in the case of an emergency, especially if communications systems are down.

4.6 EMERGENCY LESSONS TO EDUCATE YOUR KIDS

Toddlers aren't yet mature enough to be left on their own. But even at this young age, you might start forming the habit of Everyday Carry (EDC) the necessities. Young toddlers often mimic what they see adults doing. Consequently, if you put on your EDC every morning (keys, phone, wallet, etc.), you may provide young toddlers and newborns with safe items for their own EDC. Items include a key, a phone, and a toy flashlight. Their "play" EDC gear may be swapped out for actual working gear as they become older and more mature. Because many kids are terrified of the darkness, torches make a great everyday carry item for kids of all ages. Having their own light teaches kids to be responsible while also giving them self-assurance and a feeling of security if they're setting up camp in the backyard, taking out the garbage after dark, doing homework late at night, or coping with a power cut. No matter what you give, be sure your youngster can't get the battery compartment since batteries may be quite harmful to small children.

Taking into consideration your maturity level, age, and experience, consider the following:

- The **Rechargeable Torch** is perfect for pupils in elementary school since it is almost indestructible and recharges without batteries by turning a hand crank. For kids in middle and high school, the Pocket torch keychain is an excellent option for illuminating their way through the night.

- Whether it's a pair of fake **keys** for a newborn or toddler or a genuine house key on a keychain or necklace linked to their bag, kids of all age groups may get used to holding and also being prepared for keys as part of their EDC. It's an essential activity that will help children now and in the future as adults. Mobile phones are obviously not appropriate for young children in the early elementary grades, but there are plenty of imitation cellular phones that your child may get used to using as part of their EDC.

- Your obsolete **mobile phone** may even be carried by elementary school pupils just for emergency calls. Charge them by keeping an eye on the battery's life and delivering it to you for recharging on a regular basis. Even a phone without mobile phone service can call 9-1-1 in an emergency. They could even simulate phoning your phone number and the numbers of reliable family members. For smaller kids, consider using a walkie-talkie for checking in and communicating as they go about the yard or neighborhood. You may supplement your child's EDC gear as you see suitable.

- Children should always have a **whistle** in their everyday carry. If they get separated from you while out on a walk or engaging in another outside activity, or in an emergency, such as when someone attempts to take them while they're playing in the yard, you may teach them to stay put and blow the whistle. The Coghlan's Quadruple Function Whistle is the best option for kids in primary school and higher. Included are the compass, whistle, magnifying lens, and thermometer.

- Excellent addition to a child's everyday carry is the **bandana**, or Shemagh, which may be used for many purposes, including protecting one's nose and mouth from the fumes produced by a campfire, transporting kindling and water, carrying snacks like fruit and nuts, and even making one's own bandage for something like a broken arm.

- A **compass** might be useful if your youngster gets lost while out walking or in the woods. Make sure youngsters understand how to operate the compass correctly and that you've checked it for accuracy before they need to use it in an emergency. It's always good to have an emergency signaling device like a whistle and some spare cash on hand in case someone needs a ride home or to a business meeting.

- **Individual hygiene** is crucial. Sunscreen, Chapstick or lip moisturizer, itching relief cream for insect bites, and so forth. Provide an EpiPen or a tablet pack with a single dose of allergy medicine for older children who have food or other serious allergies.

- If your kid is old enough and confident enough, you may have them add a **fire Stryker** or waterproof container with matches.

As parents, we must devote our whole lives to preparing our children for the worst-case scenarios they may face in the future. However, it is feasible to do so in daily life without alarming people. You could begin by teaching them basic things while they are young and gradually introduce more complex concepts as you go. No matter what happens, your child will be more capable of managing themselves with a little planning and guidance.

Chapter 5:

HOME DEFENSE

Home protection is something that everyone should consider, and preppers have much more reasons to do so than the typical person. There is always a chance that thieves may target your house in regular times because they desire good things but are too sluggish or foolish to work for them. But what will happen after the SHTF?

Consider the following case: Even though you've been struck by a catastrophe, you're doing OK. You're well-fed and hydrated, thank goodness. In order to survive without electricity, either you've converted your house to work without it, or you have a power source of your own. However, you have the means to go through this.

There's a problem, however. People are suffering all around you. Your property isn't only a target since some thug can't afford to purchase his own laptop; the majority of people consider it as a need for survival. Regardless of whether you aid your neighbors or refugees, you can't allow them to breach into your home and steal your resources.

You must be able to protect your house and everything in it if someone comes knocking.

5.1 PROTECTING ONE'S OWN PROPERTY

Uninvited visitors are deterred from entering a property by a fence, which clearly delineates the boundaries between outside and inside.

If you have the money, you can construct a costly and unsightly security fence to keep the intruders away. However, this isn't an option for the average person.

Barbed wire fencing may be cut or climbed, but it does serve as a barrier and deter casual visitors from entering the property.

Anything that slows down an assault, even if it's only by one second, is worthwhile, even if someone isn't discouraged.

Your lawn and surroundings may be able to provide you an edge over a prospective assailant, depending on your scenario. The term "tactical landscaping" refers to the practice of reducing the number of hiding spots and cover points available to would-be thieves. When they have fewer choices, you have a better idea of where they'll be when the time comes. Make the required adjustments to your life if one of your children's bedroom windows is the simplest point of access and entrance.

5.2 DOORS AND WINDOWS SECURITY

Only two locations—doors and windows—need to be secured in order to keep attackers from your real residence. About ten windows and three entrances, plus the garage door, are standard in a typical house.

- **Window security**

Windows are one of the most difficult aspects of home security to deal with. A thief may simply get in via any of these locations.

To make it a little more difficult for anybody attempting to get into your house, there are a number of things you should and can do.

   o   Blinds or curtains should be fitted in every window in your home (and used). Criminals are interested in your house to determine if it is worth their while to break in.

- o Ensuring your windows are secured with high-quality locks is the first step. An invader will try to stealthily open a window before shattering the glass.

- o The standard nylon screens are included with most windows. You may swap out those screens with more durable metal ones. Once again, this won't deter them, but all of these security precautions could cause them to reconsider their intentions.

- o It's a good idea to put security film on any windows that may serve as entry points. While it won't stop a burglar who is determined to break into your house, it will prevent the glass from breaking and make it considerably more difficult for them.

- o Alarms for windows and motion sensors work well as deterrents. Consider what a burglar would do if an alarm went off while they were fiddling with your window. They would quickly leave after doing their business with themselves.

- **Door security**

Deadbolts are wonderful. Almost everyone already has them. Most likely, 12" to 34" steel screws are used to secure your door and frame. With a little work, they are not hard to disassemble. Online or at your neighborhood home improvement shop, you may buy fairly basic reinforcement kits. By protecting the door jamb using steel and increasing the thickness of the screws that hold the entire thing together, using one of these kits could make your door framework much more secure and will make it much more difficult for an intruder to pick your lock. Installing one of these kits is a simple weekend home improvement job that won't set you back a lot of money but will make a significant difference in your level of safety.

The majority of robbers who enter via the front door, nevertheless, won't pick up or cut the lock. To accomplish this, they will bribe you into opening the doorway for them. This entails making a fake delivery person or neighbor appearance. The burglar will pretend to be someone you would answer the door for, even if they were a stranger, such as a delivery guy bringing you a box or a police officer. Once the lock is opened, they are battling the person who opened the door rather than a lock to get inside. The thieves will likely enter if the individual is an elderly woman. You are thus your front door's most crucial line of defense. In these circumstances, a surveillance camera or a spyglass is crucial. Generally speaking, go with your instincts. Do not answer the door for anybody who is in your doorway and banging if you do not even feel comfortable with them. Speak to them via the door if necessary. They will usually give up fast if you exhibit any resistance by refusing to open it.

5.3 TRAPS AND WEAPONS

You don't need a license to possess a gun in the United States. If you're not a criminal, it's a legally guaranteed right. A concealed carry or other weapons training and safety course are recommended for those who are new to the practice of guns. This must be emphasized at all costs.

Owning a gun is only as safe as the knowledge of the person who will use it. Owners that are competent only pose a threat when they want to. It's harmful to have a firearm owner who doesn't know how to use it, and it's dangerous to have one.

Train yourself: Maintain a consistent schedule of practice. Marksmanship is a vanishing art form. Having a firearm is both a privilege and a duty. Training with firearms teaches you to be your best self on the worst possible day.

5.3.1 KEEP YOUR FIREARMS SECURE YET ACCESSIBLE

On the market, there are various safes that provide rapid opening options while yet being secure. They're a must-have if you have small children with whom you don't feel comfortable trusting with weapons. Bio-ID, such as a fingerprint scan, may access certain digital locks. Make sure it works every time you use it if you buy one. Only around 60% of the time does the finger scanner on my mobile function. If you're going to use a gun, you want to make sure it works 100% of the time. Make a few comparisons. Find a method that works for you.

Understand how your house is laid out. Sheetrock may be pierced by bullets like paper. First and foremost, make sure you know where your child's room is located before deciding to use a firearm. Do you recall the activity when you were supposed to seek blind spots all throughout your house? For firing angles, do the same. Is there anything you might expect to see when you exit your bedroom and point a pistol at it? Surely not! How about one more bed for a member of the family? Where can you hide if a thief comes after you with a gun? Are you exposed in any way? When you tread on a creaky location in your house, what does it sound like? What is the typical response time of the police in your area?

Who can protect the elderly members of the family? Who has the weapon? Is it possible for them to get to it in a timely manner? Young children, in particular, need both a hiding location and an escape route. Bathtubs are a great hiding area in the home.

Children are most likely to be safest in a tub surrounded by hard stuff if bullets are flying.

5.3.2 THE BEST WEAPON FOR SELF-DEFENSE AT HOME

You need a firearm that you are comfortable handling. You should always use the gun you have the greatest familiarity with and the most repetitions with. That's all there is to it. Loading, operating, and removing clogs should be second nature to you. When the need to use lethal force to defend oneself arises, you must depend on muscle memory rather than knowledge of how a particular gun works.

All other things being equal, you would like a firearm that is efficient at a close distance and does not over-penetrate when used in your own house. An "over-penetrate" is a term that refers to anything that goes past a wall or target and continues. Intruders, walls, and even loved ones might all be in danger of being struck by a gunshot if it travels through them and continues to anything beyond them.

Guns are just like any other piece of equipment. The right tools are required for certain tasks. You can't compare an orbital sander to a flathead screwdriver since they're not the same tool. Make sure you're using the correct tool for the task at hand.

5.3.3 FIREARM RULES

These cannot be negotiated. Every competent user of a weapon should be able to recall these four safety guidelines on demand.

- Unless you're prepared to destroy the target, never aim a gun at it. Consider the possibility that the gun's muzzle will emit a fatal laser beam. Don't cross the phantom beams over other individuals. Keep the firearm always aimed downwards.
- One must always carry a loaded gun. I don't care if you're absolutely certain it isn't. Always treat it as though it's loaded with live ammunition, and the protection is disengaged. You may see what happens when a person uses a weapon they think is unloaded in Netflix's very popular series, Tiger King.
- Until you're prepared to shoot, don't touch the trigger. The weapon's ultimate safety is you. When you have your finger on the trigger of a firearm, it is quite simple to accidentally discharge it, particularly if you are in an extremely stressful scenario.
- Always keep an eye on both your aim and what's behind it. This might be people, things, or any combination thereof. You run the risk of missing your target. Even if the bullet misses the target entirely, it will continue on its way.

More guidelines are provided below, and it is highly advised that you follow them.

- o If you're a parent, you bear exclusive responsibility for the well-being of your children. Teaching your children firearm safety and making it clear that weapons can be dangerous if mishandled is an important part of this. When not in use, keep firearms stored safely.

- o Don't shoot warning shots, no matter how high they fly. When a bullet goes up, it also comes down, and you never know where or what it will hit when it does. A person's reaction to seeing a gun isn't going to change if it's fired.

- o Do not aim at a target on the opposite side of a door while firing. EVER. Many individuals have mistakenly killed their family members by shooting through open doors.

- o Don't reveal the details of your weapons to anybody. Thieves are drawn to it.

5.4 PROTECTING GARAGE

A house may be broken into extremely quickly via the garage door. To avoid being seen by the neighbors, robbers prefer to break into a home through the back door, where there is less possibility of being seen. Utilizing a wood piece to pry open a small gap in the doorway and a clothes hanger to release the latch makes it simple to enter. You may think of it as the same thing as using an actual slim-jim to open a vehicle door. A skilled thief could break into a home via the garage in 20 to 30 seconds flat if they practiced their craft well beforehand.

Typically, the garage lock is suspended from a rope that is relatively easy to release. With only a few pounds of pressure, they may latch onto the strings, or anything attached to it, or even the locking mechanism itself. Remove any tags that are still present from the string. The cable may be completely removed if you choose, but it should, at the absolute least, be reduced so that it can't be manually pulled on by being pushed to the wedges in the top of the garage.

Using a zip tie, you may secure the lock if you intend to be gone from your house for a long period of time. To strengthen the garage door's top, use a 2x4. Metals that are flexible, like aluminum, are often used to make garage doors. By adding a piece of wood to reinforce it, you eliminate any flex and make it much more difficult to wedge open. You may use an additional board or material to cover the gap at the top, making it hard for a coat hanger to pass through.

5.5 USE A DOG AS A SECURITY

When humans first domesticated dogs, they were wolves that had been genetically modified by selective breeding. About 15,000 years ago, humans began interacting with dogs. Dogs and humans have coexisted for as long as people have known how to plant seeds, add water, and watch for growth. Since the dawn of time, dogs and humans have collaborated on many projects.

It is hard for humans to fully appreciate a dog's sense of scent. In the past, I've known a guy who worked as a drug-sniffing dog trainer. As he put it, it's like baking a cake; you smell cake. Every food that can be smelled by a dog is. For example, a dog that is trained to smell out narcotics can identify even the most microscopic amounts of drugs in plastic bags, coffee cans loaded with coffee, duffel bags, the trunk of a vehicle, and more with only a few sniffs. A few dogs can even identify malignant cells and low glucose levels after being trained.

More than 4 times as far as humans can hear, a dog's hearing is more sensitive, and it can spin its ears almost 180 degrees to locate the source of a sound.

Dog owners who have also ordered pizza may relate. A dog's job is to protect you and your family from danger. A dog will bark and make a lot of noise if someone is approaching your house before you do. Dog, mailman, or serial murderer might be the culprit. They don't give a damn. They'll make a big deal out of it and let you know exactly what's going on.

In addition, they have a mouthful of sharp things and jaws with frighteningly powerful jaw muscles, so be careful around them. A Labrador Retriever's biting strength is 230 pounds on average. Not everyone is capable of doing this, let alone biting that hard. When compared to a canine's bite, a person's bite is only approximately half as powerful as that of a dog. Dogs are carnivorous. They have the skills and the construction to rip the flesh off the bone.

If you're a dog lover, chances are you already own one or more. This is a great opportunity to obtain a dog if you've always wanted one but never had the chance. Chihuahuas can't win fights, but if you've ever met one, you'll know that they'll go toe-to-toe with someone 40 times their size.

Chapter 6:

OFF GRID LIVING

A little piece of land may be transformed into a never-ending source of wealth if the correct amount of courage, problem-solving abilities, and survival knowledge is used. Being able to live off-grid and cultivate a more environmentally friendly style of life appeals to many people. You may reduce your impact on the planet, discover how to be completely self-sufficient, and enjoy the numerous benefits of Mother Nature by adopting a more natural lifestyle. Living off the land, however, is not for the faint of heart or those who lack the necessary preparation. To be able to live (and prosper) without municipal utilities, food shops, and other necessities that we take for granted on a daily basis requires years of preparation and practice.

6.1 RESOURCES OF NATURAL ELECTRICITY FOR OFF-GRID HOMES

One of the most convenient things about living in the United States is that power outages don't happen very often. A power outage, on the other hand, may mean no electricity or heat for those who live completely off the grid. Hours or even days might be required for it. When a utility provider goes down, it may be quite inconvenient for anybody who has to be without power for a long period of time until they get everything back up and running.

In the event of a power outage, several natural sources of electricity may help keep off-grid homes powered. Alternative or renewable energy choices include geothermal cooling and heating, solar photovoltaic systems (PV), wind turbines, and micro-hydro power systems, just to name a few.

6.2 OFF-GRID POWER?

An energy source that may be used to generate electricity is off-grid power. Instead of relying on external resources, this kind of system is able to generate its own energy.

6.3 WHAT DO BATTERY PACKS DO?

High-amperage DC power is provided by battery packs, which are made up of a grouping of batteries wired together. Solar and wind-powered battery packs may be used later on when renewable energy sources run low. Battery packs have been designed to be difficult to ignite while yet being able to provide a significant quantity of power. In most cases, battery packs are used in combination with an inverter/charger unit and are charged by solar panels or wind turbines. Even if it isn't available at the time, this ensures sufficient energy storage for future use.

When the batteries are fully charged, they may be used to power AC-powered appliances and devices like lights and televisions. A battery pack may be used with any off-grid system designed for it, including boat or RV power systems, and has several advantages over other energy storage methods. As a result, you don't need to carry an additional inverter/charger device, which saves money and space.

Solar panels and wind turbines can't be damaged if their batteries run out or if they don't get enough sunlight or wind to recharge during the day since battery packs provide a backup power source.

6.4 WIND TURBINES

Wind turbines may be used to generate electricity for off-grid residences that are located near bodies of water (such as lakes). The natural energy created by airflow is captured by wind turbines. Turbines generate electricity when there is enough wind. Wind power is a renewable source of energy that may be found in the vast majority of North America. When solar or geothermal systems aren't an option for off-grid homes in remote areas, this makes it an excellent choice.

Wind turbines provide a number of advantages.

- Because they don't need a lot of upkeep, they are a good investment.
- Even if there isn't enough sunshine or water for solar panels, they can still be used to generate electricity. As a result, off-grid dwellings located in remote areas may benefit more from this kind of system than dwellings located near readily available natural resources like sunlight and fresh water.

Wind turbines, on the other hand, are not without their drawbacks.

- You might want to consider spreading out your purchases to reduce the initial outlay since they can be rather costly to install and need a large amount of floor space.
- There is a downside, though, to the high levels of noise associated with these systems.

6.5 SOLAR PHOTOVOLTAIC (PV) SYSTEMS

Another kind of renewable energy that may be used to power off-grid homes is solar photovoltaic

(PV) systems. Systems of this kind capture solar energy and transform it into usable electric power. It is possible to install solar photovoltaic (PV) systems that are either connected to the grid or off it. When solar power is fed into a utility grid, other customers may use it, too. This is called a "grid-tied" system. In order to keep their local utility company connected while maintaining their own power source, people might choose a grid-tied system.

On the other hand, off-grid systems use solar panels to generate electricity, which is then used to power the home or property. In order to use these types of systems, they must be paired with a power storage system, such as a battery pack.

The advantages of photovoltaic systems are many.

- In addition to being very quick and easy to install, these devices may be used with or without battery packs to store energy.
- To put it another way, they provide clean energy that doesn't add to global warming. Because we know that climate change will continue to affect the planet in devastating ways, this is very critical.

However, there are also some disadvantages:

- The cost of solar panels, both to buy and install, is rather high.
- When the weather is very hot or cold, photovoltaic systems don't operate as well because they are less efficient in converting sunlight into energy.
- Your property's exposure to sunlight throughout the year may make these kinds of systems impractical, depending on where you live.

Homeowners who live in remote areas where access to standard utility networks is either impossible or impractical might rely on solar and wind power systems. Turbines may be used to generate electricity from the wind if you live near a lake, ocean, stream, or other body of water that does not freeze during the winter months.

6.6 SMALL-SCALE HYDRO SYSTEMS

Micro-hydro, an alternative renewable energy system, is becoming more popular for off-grid homes. A stream or river near your home may provide renewable power via the use of these systems, which collect energy from flowing water. Micro-hydro systems can still power your home even if there isn't, but you'll need to reroute rainwater into the stream or river that leads to your hydroelectric turbine from another source.

The energy generated when flowing liquid turns blades connected to an axle is used to power water turbines. Conveniently, the axle is connected to an electric generator, which generates electricity that can be used in your home or business.

With a micro-hydro system, there are a number of advantages.

- The lower initial investment and ease of maintenance compared to other renewable energy choices make them an excellent choice.

- Even if there isn't a lot of sunshine or wind, they can still be used. Solar panels, wind turbines, or both can't be installed in remote areas because of this.

If you're considering employing micro-hydro systems to power your home, you'll need to keep in mind a few drawbacks before making a final decision.

- Although they don't need much maintenance, they may be rather expensive to purchase, and you must take special precautions to ensure that the water turbine blades are not damaged.

- The installation of these systems requires a large amount of space, which is not ideal if your property is already overcrowded or has a limited amount of available space.

6.7 SETUP OF YOUR OFF-GRID DWELLING FOR OPTIMUM POWER CONSUMPTION

a) Consider the amount of electricity each appliance consumes and where it might be located to maximize efficiency while setting up an off-grid home. Using these recommendations will help ensure that the power generated by any solar panels or other renewable energy sources you have access to is used as efficiently as possible to power your appliances.

b) The most direct sunlight during the day should be received by solar panels.

c) If you're sending your excess energy back into the grid, use high-efficiency inverters.

d) When possible, use LED or CFL lights instead of conventional choices. Because they use less power, they generate more excess energy at peak hours.

e) The sun's rays may be used to warm water for bathing and other purposes.

f) Analyze whether you really need any tools at all. As an example, if your fireplace is not in use during the winter months and you are off-grid, it is preferable to keep the chimney closed to reduce the amount of heat lost from the house.

g) You may also cook on a solar oven instead of a stove if you have the money to do so.

h) To cook, use a bonfire rather than a stove.

i) Make sure your appliances aren't using electricity when you don't need them by setting the timers on them.

j) Drive a pump that circulates hot air around the house or use it for other heating purposes with the help of your waterpower.

k) Cold tap water may be warmed before it enters your tank using solar heat collectors.

l) Make sure you are not exceeding the maximum output capacity of your solar panel or other renewable energy sources while using all the appliances in your home by keeping track of the power consumption of each one (measured in watts) to identify potential problems. Consider installing more windows or using a different power source, such as wind turbines, during peak hours when demand is at its highest.

m) The initial step in prepping might be the most challenging. It's difficult to plan ahead when you don't know how long you'll want supplies or what sort of emergencies you could encounter. It is critical, however, to begin by selecting an energy source and then working backward from there.

Chapter 7:

FIRST AID FOR PREPPERS

Affected areas usually only suffer material loss when disasters strike. You or a loved one may be hurt, and you may be able to get medical attention for them. First aid supplies are an essential part of preparing yourself for a disaster and learning how to become self-sufficient thereafter. There will be times when you and your loved ones will need to use these instruments, so be ready to help if someone does. After reading this chapter, you will have a better understanding of what you should include in the first aid kit, where to use the instruments, and what you may use in place of certain medications and materials. In addition, you'll learn some basic first aid skills.

7.1 SURVIVAL MEDICINE BASICS

When you're in a situation where you can't rely on outside help, survival medicine is your only option. Isolation, lack of infrastructure, or overcrowding in medical facilities are all possibilities. With survival medicine, you're able to care for yourself or another person until you're able to seek treatment from qualified medical experts who have earned advanced degrees and are well-stocked medical facilities. That might take some time.

My finest and most basic bit of advice is; *Know what's in your first aid kit.*

If you don't already have one, I strongly advise that you do so immediately. It makes no difference which one you choose. The more you study, the more you'll be able to add and change. Take a peek inside your emergency preparedness kit as soon as possible if you have one. In other words, you need to know what's in there, why you need it, and how to use everything.

In the event of an emergency, you must be able to locate scissors and gauze even if your eyes are closed. You never know when you'll be in a circumstance when you are forced to rely on your ability to see to find what you require and how to utilize it.

7.2 MEDICAL TOOLS

When it comes to preparing for an emergency, it's best to begin by using the supplies you already have at home. These instruments are recommended for treating small traumatic injuries that often occur during routine housework. Burns, Cuts, Splinters, and Sting Injuries are all included in this list. When disaster strikes, it is a good idea to include the tools necessary to treat these injuries in your survival pack in case they arise.

It's important to have a well-stocked first aid kit on hand in case of minor accidents or emergencies. Always have a first-aid kit on hand, both at home and on the go. Keep your supplies out of the range of youngsters but easily accessible. Kids of legal age should be made aware of the existence and purpose of the kits.

First-aid kits may be purchased at most drugstores, or you can make your own. There are a variety of ways in which you may customize your gear. Included in a basic first-aid kit may be:

- Laxative
- Antacids
- Glue stick
- Sticky tape
- Thermometer
- First-aid guide

- Soap and water
- Antibiotic cream
- Aloe vera lotion
- Calamine cream
- Eyewash mixture
- A pad or eye shield
- Quick-chill packets
- Tweezers and scissors
- Topical hydrocortisone
- Medicine to treat diarrhea
- Cold and cough remedies
- Elastic bandages that wrap
- Various sizes of safety pins
- Wipes and antiseptic solution
- Broad triangle-shaped bandage
- Finger brace made of aluminum
- Plastic bags in a variety of sizes
- A lubricant such as petroleum jelly
- Spoon, medication cup, or syringe
- Breathing restriction (surgical mask)
- Cotton-tipped swabs and cotton balls
- Use of hydrogen peroxide for cleaning
- Sterile saline for flushing and irrigation
- A 16-french catheter or rubber tourniquet
- Such as diphenhydramine, an antihistamine
- Sterile nonstick bandages and various sizes of roller gauze
- Medication for personal use that doesn't need refrigeration
- Epinephrine auto-injector if your doctor has recommended one
- Several pairs of disposable examination gloves made without latex
- To flush wounds, use a turkey baster or another bulb suction device
- Painkillers like acetaminophen (Tylenol, among others) and ibuprofen
- Bandages in different sizes and bandage strips in the shape of butterflies

This kit may be purchased at any well-stocked medicine store, but you'll have to put it together yourself. Remember to pack the items in a clear, resealable nylon bag when you're done. There is no need to purchase a specific case as long as the bag is water-resistant. Adhesives and sterilized items must be kept dry at all times. In light of the size of this collection, it's a good idea to label and categories everything. Each category of items may be placed in a smaller bag and then placed in a larger backpack. This way, you'll be able to keep everything organized and often check to see whether you need to restock any of your supplies.

7.3 KEEPING YOUR FIRST AID SUPPLIES UPDATED

At least twice a year, check to make sure the contents of your basic aid kit are updated and in good working order. Sanitize the bag where you keep all your equipment and non-packaged utensils, too, on this occasion. Expect to remove everything from the bag, then spray it with a disinfectant. Spray the tweezers, scissors, and anything else that can resist moisture while you wait for the bag to dry out. Then go through the rest of the items to see if there is anything that needs to be discarded or replaced. This is another reason why it's so vital to label everything. You may also create a checklist with labels so that you don't forget to restock your kit with any necessary items. Seal the individual packages and inspect the contents, especially if the item contains an adhesive or medication. If any of them has holes or moisture in them, they are not safe to use on or near an open wound. You should get rid of them and get some new ones.

You should be able to use the majority of your equipment for years to come if you store it in a watertight, puncture-proof, and drop-resistant bag. Bandages, gauzes, and other metal tools have a near-infinite life duration. Even the ones that can't be used for a long time after their expiration date may be used for a short time. The same may be said for the majority of over-the-counter medications. While most pharmaceuticals have an expiration date of 15 to 60 months after production, this doesn't always mean that they can't be used after that period has passed. The expiration date, on the other hand, takes storage and handling into account.

If, for example, the pharmacist removes the medication from its original package and moves it into another container, this may have an impact on the drug's potency, life duration, and safety, among other things. You should keep your first aid kit's medication in manufacturer-sealed packaging for stress-free handling.

Even beyond the expiration date, most over-the-counter medications in tablet or capsule form don't lose potency for 3-5 years if they are kept in an unopened container. Liquid medications are a different matter since they are made with extra substances that might become unstable beyond their expiration date. Consequently, they are not as stable as solid medications. First, if you have any fluids in your kit, whether they are medications, disinfectants, or anything else — check them first. It's time to replace them if they become unclear, discolored, thick or liquid, or smell terrible. Antibiotics and sip-pens are the two most notable exceptions to the rule that prevents their use beyond the expiration date. Epinephrine, the active ingredient in pi-pens, degrades rapidly beyond the expiration date. The same is true for antibiotics, which, even if left unopened and stored in a cold, dark, and dry location, will degrade within a few months after their expiration date. Antibiotics may only be used for a few weeks or months, regardless of their stated expiration date, even if they are opened. Your first aid pack should include unopened tablets and capsules of antibiotics. Spray antibiotics may be used, but they must be replaced six months after they have been opened. It's not safe to use them on an open wound.

7.4 THE MOST IMPORTANT EMERGENCY MEDICAL PROCEDURES

There are a variety of ways you might be injured, depending on the nature of the disaster. Even if you aren't hit by falling debris, fire, or water, the fear and anxiety that occurs during an emergency may still lead to an injury. You may be ready for these scenarios, whether they involve you or someone you care about, by learning the basics of basic first aid.

Prioritizing the "Three P's" is one of the most important aspects of first aid.

- Preserve life
- Promote recovery
- Prevent further harm

While these objectives may seem quite straightforward when someone you love is hurt, worry might make it easy to forget what you need to perform to assist them. How to implement the Three Ps is shown here.

7.4.1 PREVENTING BLEEDING

While it's crucial to stop the bleeding, take care of the following procedures first.

- If you have disposable gloves, put those on or clean your hands beforehand. This will shield you against contagious illnesses that may be transmitted via a person's blood, such as viral hepatitis and HIV/AIDS.
- Wrap the injury with gauze or cloth (e.g., blanket, towel, clothing).
- Direct pressure should be used to halt the blood flow and promote coagulation.
- If you can, raise the area of the body that is bleeding above the person's head.
- If the cloth becomes wet, do not remove it. The clotting process will be hampered by removing the top layer, increasing blood loss. Instead, if additional layers are required, add them.
- After the bleeding stops, apply a fresh bandage to the wound.

Get medical assistance if:

- The injury is severe.
- There is ongoing bleeding.
- You suspect arterial bleeding.
- The sides of the wound are widely spaced.
- Bandages have blood seeping through them.
- Animal or human bites are to blame for the damage.
- The damage is a burn, a puncture, or an electrical wound.
- Once pressure has been applied, the wound begins to seep blood.

If you're driving the patient to the hospital, ensure someone else can take care of the wound while you're driving.

7.4.2 TREATING BURNS

The sole treatment for minor burns is to administer cold water to the affected area, and after it has cooled down, apply an ointment to keep it moist. Avoid breaking the blisters and keep the wound away from direct sunlight. A person who has had a serious burn will need medical assistance as soon as possible. To prevent infection, don't put anything on the wound; instead, cover it with loose material. Give the injured person medicine to relieve their discomfort if they are in excruciating agony.

7.4.3 SCRAPES AND CUTS

As soon as someone begins bleeding excessively, the first thing you should do is prevent them from losing blood. As quickly as possible, locate a bandage or clean cloth and apply it directly to the wound. Check to see whether the bleeding has stopped after 20 to 30 minutes of keeping the bandage on the wound. If so, clean the wound by gently cleaning it with a towel dipped in water and an antiseptic. Don't wash open wounds with soap. Spray an antibiotic solution on the wound before covering it with a bandage. Never spray or apply medicine to a cut that seems too deep or won't stop bleeding. Cover it loosely with a towel to prevent contamination. Maintain your pressure while seeking medical attention. Simple nosebleeds may be treated by having the person lean forward and press a piece of fabric over their nose until the bleeding stops.

7.4.4 TREATING BITES FROM SNAKES AND INSECTS

Bee stings may be quite painful, yet for many individuals, they are merely a minor inconvenience. A sting, however, may be fatal for those who have a venom allergy.

It's crucial to always keep an eye out for an allergic response after a bee sting since an allergy might manifest at any moment.

Following are symptoms of an allergic response to a sting:

- Hives
- Itching
- Flushing
- The swelling moving from the sting site.
- Indicators of anaphylaxis (a potentially fatal allergic response that may result in breathing difficulties, blue lips and nails, perspiration, disorientation, and hives).

If you see any symptoms of an allergic response to a bee sting, call 911 right once or take the victim to the hospital. It's best to have an EpiPen on hand for anybody who is allergic to bee stings.

While giving first aid to a person who doesn't have a known allergy to bees, keep an eye out for any symptoms of an allergy:

- Remove the stinger right away. To prevent it from stinging the human with additional venom, this must take place. It doesn't matter what approach you use; what matters is that you do this promptly.

- Use soap and water to clean the area.

- Apply a cold compress to the area to reduce swelling but avoid touching the skin with ice.

- To lessen swelling and itching, use an antihistamine or allergy medicine (like Benadryl).

- For pain, use Tylenol or Advil (ibuprofen).

7.4.5 FROSTBITE

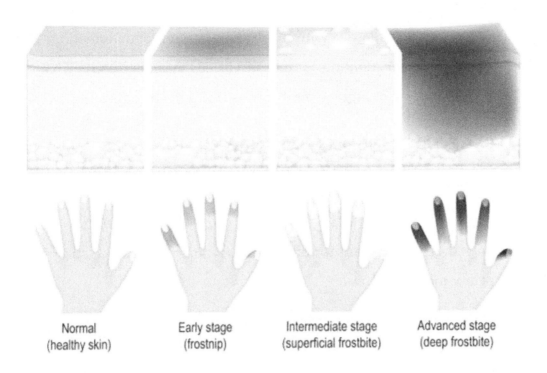

| Normal (healthy skin) | Early stage (frostnip) | Intermediate stage (superficial frostbite) | Advanced stage (deep frostbite) |

When the body's tissues are exposed to extreme cold, frostbite may result. Even while this harms your skin in the exact opposite way to a burn, the effects are almost identical.

The damaged region must be gently and gradually warmed in order to treat frostbite. It should only be carried out by a medical specialist, if at all feasible.

You can start first aid for frostbite if that isn't feasible or while you're waiting for an ambulance.

- Leave the chilly area.

- For 25 to 30 minutes, soak the afflicted region in warm water.

- Avoid rubbing the injured region.

- Avoid using dry heat sources like fireplaces and heating pads. After your fingers and toes have heated up, you may lay clean cotton balls among them.

- Wrap the area loosely with bandages.

- For pain, use Tylenol or Advil (ibuprofen).
- Seek medical help as soon as you can.

You may also reheat the region with skin-to-skin contact (placing your skin against another person's) for moderate frostbite on smaller areas.

7.4.6 HEATSTROKE

Your body has a preferred temperature, which just so happens to be the temperature at which you feel most at ease or a few degrees over what we refer to as "room temperature." Long-term exposure to high temperatures and inadequate hydration may result in heatstroke. Headaches, nausea, vomiting, dizziness, muscle cramps, a weak pulse, profuse sweating, and chilly skin are all signs of heat exhaustion. Transfer the individual to a shaded area. At the very least, cover them with something to prevent the light if you are unable to move them. Give them water in little doses and cover their foreheads with a cold towel. You may gradually lower their body temperature in this manner.

7.4.7 HYPOTHERMIA

A condition of the body brought on by extended exposure to cold temperatures. Shivering, poor coordination, slurred speech, loss of consciousness, and red, icy skin are just a few of its symptoms. Move the body out of the cold, or until you can move them, cover them with blankets and heat packs. Be very cautious while doing this since any sudden movement in their body might result in cardiac arrest. Avoid applying heat directly to their skin in order to prevent burning them. Give them warm drinks if they are still aware. Avoid placing the person on the chilly ground and remove their clothes if they are wet.

7.4.8 FRACTURES AND SPRAINS

It might be difficult to distinguish between fractures and sprains. It's more likely a broken bone than a simple sprain if the affected body part appears strange, cannot be moved, or if the pain persists even after a few hours. Sprains often heal on their own, but there are techniques to make the healing process easier. Applying ice, which constricts blood vessels and reduces blood flow, is one way to do this. To prevent the bag of ice from coming into contact with the sensitive skin, wrap it in fabric. Ice the injury for a little while, then relax and repeat the ice. Maintain the area's elevation and refrain from adding weight to it. You may use a splint to stabilize the bones and prevent movement if you suspect someone of having a broken bone. Try not to move the bones since doing so might do more damage than benefit. Give the person who was injured an ice pack to put on the injured area and anti-inflammatory medication.

7.4.9 TREATING INFECTION

One of the fatal things that humans have ever encountered is an infected wound. Several tiny critters will attempt to establish a presence in a damaged location. For a long time, people died from these diseases without antibiotics, which is one of the greatest medical breakthroughs in human history. However, as a layman, you sadly have very little control over infections.

If a patient exhibits any of the listed signs and symptoms, a wound may be infected:

- Fever
- A foul stench was coming from my region of injury.
- Skin that is red, puffy, painful, or heated around the incision site.
- When the wound should have healed, blood or pus is oozing out of it.

The best way to treat this condition is by a doctor; therefore, if one of the symptoms appears, get immediate medical attention:

- Numbness
- Unbearable ache
- Respiration difficulty
- Uncontrollable bleeding
- Suffering chills or a fever
- Abnormally rapid heartbeat
- Bewilderment and uncertainty
- The wound seems itself opening again
- Red slashes emerging from the area of injury

To acquire a diagnosis and medication for these illnesses, you'll need to consult a doctor first. Without the right treatment, you can lose a limb or perhaps your life.

Chapter 8:

NATURAL MEDICINE

Herbal or natural medicine has roots in prehistoric societies. It entails the use of plants as medicines to cure illness and improve people's overall health and wellness. Some plants should be used with the same degree of care as pharmaceutical drugs because they contain potent (strong) components. In actuality, many pharmaceutical drugs are man-made derivatives of naturally occurring plant components. For instance, the foxglove plant was used to create the cardiac medication digitalis.

8.1 ADVANTAGES OF NATURAL MEDICINE

Natural medicine offers several useful advantages:

- You don't need a doctor's approval to purchase these items, nor do you need to depend on a multibillion-dollar pharmaceutical firm to manufacture them. Many herbal remedies may be produced at home using ingredients from your garden, and they aren't subject to strict regulations.

- Due to medical regulations and the company's R&D efforts to develop it, they don't cost a leg and an arm.
- In contrast to new medications, which undergo several years of clinical testing before being made available to the general public, herbs have undergone centuries of testing. What doesn't work, what works, and what hazards are all known to us?

Numerous important medicinal products come from organic plant sources. For instance, the active component of aspirin was first found in the willow tree's leaves. Blood clotting, reducing fever, and managing pain are just a few conditions for which aspirin is currently utilized. Oxycontin, a painkiller, is chemically identical to opium, the main substance in the poppy flower, which physicians administered excessively.

Herbs are highly helpful, particularly for the common, everyday difficulties that everyone sometimes faces; however, they cannot address all of your problems. For instance, no herb may be used in place of insulin. I don't want to overstate the potential of herbs. Even if they are wonderful, no plant on earth can replace a transplant of bone marrow or remove a cataract.

8.2 GROWN-YOUR-OWN MEDICINAL HERBS

Another approach to being self-reliant in emergency scenarios is to grow your own medical and culinary herbs. Many plants have regenerative and healing properties. It's likely that you already have some on your spice rack. However, you may not be able to purchase them in a store after an unexpected event, like a natural disaster. Growing them is a fantastic method to ensure that you have access to them whenever you need them. The recent coronavirus pandemic has highlighted the need to have a healthy immune system. Numerous herbs may assist you with that as well as much more. You should regularly consume herbs like oregano, garlic, basil, fennel, and sage, as well as spices like pepper, cinnamon, cayenne, and cloves. Both gardens and containers may be used to cultivate these herbs. If you don't have enough space to produce your own herbs because you live in an apartment, you may also have dried beans on hand. If opened, they may be stored for approximately a year. They will maintain their healing abilities in closed containers for 12 to 18 months.

8.3 HERBS CATEGORIES

- **Apoptogenic:** reduces stress.
- **Expectorant:** reduces clogging by assisting.
- **Astringent:** bodily tissue may contract or shrink.
- **Anti-Inflammatory**: reduces edema and inflammation.
- **Culinary:** excellent for food, Aromatic fantastic for smells.
- **Digestive:** supports the natural food-processing mechanisms in your body.
- **Immunity:** aids in the immunological response of your body to fight illness.

8.4 GETTING YOUR MEDICINE CABINET READY

All of these herbs may be cultivated in your own backyard garden. All of these are used to treat typical illnesses. These are my top recommendations if you want a fully stocked medicine cabinet with supplies you can replace on your own property.

Since many of them are perennials, they grow all year round.

- **Sage**

An excellent herb for cooking, but it also has additional advantages. There is medicinal use for throat and mouth issues, particularly for scratchy throats. Sage is a common ingredient in homemade toothpaste made from herbal powders since it helps whiten teeth. Another benefit of sage is that it contains a lot of antioxidants.

- **Peppermint**

Growing peppermint plants is simple. Sometimes, it's too simple; take caution, as they might spread like weeds and encroach on neighboring fields. Stuffy sinuses and unsettled stomachs respond well to peppermint. As you are aware, it has a fantastic taste, and when mixed into water, it makes the liquid feel colder and more refreshing.

As the cooling feeling acts on the skin, it could be applied as a balm to sunburns to help ease the pain. Some people find that peppermint relieves headaches.

Additionally, it relieves nausea, particularly that brought on by pregnancy, morning sickness, or car sickness from motion.

- **Calendula**

An absolute must for skin problems. Calendula is excellent for treating fungal skin infections and rashes. When you're unwell, it helps ease pain in your lymph nodes. Depending on what you are coloring, it may also be utilized as a food or fabric dye, producing hues ranging from an intense lemon yellowish to an olive-brown. Even though not everyone like the taste, it may be hidden with other flavorings.

- **Lavender**

A lovely plant with a wonderful scent. Most well-known for being soothing. A popular choice for aromatherapy.

- **Feverfew**

This may be collected twice a year and grows quickly. Lovely addition to your yard that is also effective for headache relief.

- **Holy Basil/ Tulsi**

As an adaptogen, tulsi reduces stress. Some individuals find that it improves their concentration, helps them "get out of their brains," and makes them feel more in the moment. Tulsi has antimicrobial properties and is even a component of mouthwash. It may serve as a replacement for the familiar basil in recipes, although some people find the taste to be overpowering.

- **Elderberry**

Your greatest option for surviving the cold and flu season. It is generally known that this one supports the immune system. It contains a significant amount of vitamin C, has anti-inflammatory properties, and is a great addition to syrup or jam that you can use to top pancakes.

- **Bergamot/ Bee Balm**

If you're not cautious, this might spiral out of control like mint. Bee balm is antibacterial. This mild herb is excellent for children and is useful for stomach problems and coughs.

- **Lemon Balm**

This mint has perhaps the broadest variety of applications among its family members. Helping to reduce fevers is one of its finest applications. It's used by people to manage stress. People are often calmed down by the scent, and drinking lemon balm tea may aid in putting you or your children to sleep.

- **Hyssop**

Another plant that, if left unchecked, may take over a garden. A top choice for respiratory problems. A top selection for the flu season.

- **Chamomile**

Almost everyone loves it since it helps with gas, tastes fantastic in tea, and helps you relax and go to sleep. Making chamomile tea is popular. You won't even taste the tea if you leave it a few minutes to steep in the cup. Use more than you normally would and let it boil for a while to create a wonderful, darker color than you may be accustomed to. Great for reducing eye discomfort. Fantastic for the eyes is a used teabag.

- **Valerian**

It is most recognized for its ability to alleviate tension and promote sleep. The flowers smell wonderful. Similar to catnip, this herb is renowned for luring cats.

- **Echinacea**

Echinacea is often harvested from the roots. The length of time it takes for your echinacea to develop to a size that makes harvesting it worthwhile is thus around two years. The sooner a patch is active, the better.

Most individuals who are familiar with this plant are aware of its capacity to combat illness. Although it may be consumed, it is often used topically. The root's numbing properties make it a fantastic remedy for sore throats, even when you only chew it.

- **Oregano**

Both delicious and effective against bacteria, marinara. Antioxidants, which are essential for life, are abundant in oregano.

- **Onions and garlic**

It is one of the greatest food additives and is used in practically everything. Both garlic and fungus are resistant to it. Garlic is used sparingly for cuts and minor wounds to help them heal faster.

- **Horseradish**

Either you adore it, or you despise it. If you allow it, this plant will also spread. It is a hardy plant that doesn't need much assistance and is a well-known cure for nasal and bronchial problems as well as urethral infections.

- **Yarrow**

You may not need to plant yarrow yourself as it is so widespread in certain places. In fact, it resembles a weed. It's simple to forage for it. It is well known that it promotes blood clotting, but its greatest use is to halt bleeding. If you have a fever and are feeling hot, it may cause you to sweat, which helps to regulate body temperature.

- **Hollyhock/ Marshmallow**

Hollyhocks are a really attractive plant, as well as every part of it is delicious, so don't mistake them for the mushy white cylinders that usually melt over Graham Crackers. It is another excellent herb for calming throat, skin discomfort, and stomach since it is a mucilaginous plant. The root of a marshmallow is often harvested.

- **Wood Betony**

Excellent for treating headaches and migraines. The majority of the other plants are more resilient than this one, which prefers to thrive in shaded regions.

- **Elecampane**

The most suitable option for bronchial problems, such as coughing or wheezing.

- **Dill**

Dill is a great option for anybody with endometriosis since it may also relieve sadness and menstrual pains, according to some preliminary research.

- **Comfrey**

This shouldn't be eaten. It's harmful to you. It works well as a poultice on wounds.

- **Horehound**

The same function should be served by this plant, which is still employed in cough drops.

8.5 ESSENTIAL OILS

The "essence" of a plant is its essential oil, not because vitamins or other nutrients are equally important to your health. They are the plant's most concentrated form. You may manufacture them by grinding up a plant and then distilling the resulting liquid. The best location to store essential oils is a cold environment with containers that are sufficiently dark to protect them from excessive light exposure.

A Must-Have for Every Prepper:

It is reasonable to assume that you will not have access to carrier oils if you are in a precarious circumstance. In order to assist the dispersion of the essential oil and increase its surface area in this situation, any fat-based substance would work effectively. You may use any kind of fat, including organic jojoba oil, as long as it can be used topically and is safe to do so. Why don't we utilize water? In any case, water and oil tend to reject one another, making the topical application more challenging. Essential oils may be safely applied to the skin by mixing them with one oz of water inside a spray bottle before using. Just keep in mind that the oil won't mix with the water properly, so you may not get an equal application.

8.6 SURVIVAL MEDICATION ADVICE

You run the risk of making things worse if you don't know what you're doing.

- It doesn't always make sense just because you once saw it on television. To make their productions seem as authentic as possible, television shows and films will often use expert advisors. But they are constrained. The producers and creators of a show eventually write anything they want to keep it entertaining since it's all about entertainment. If you watch these things with a true expert, they'll be eager to explain just how many things television gets incorrect.

- When treating a patient with many people present, assign tasks to the extra hands. To raise a leg, ask them to bring a cushion. Instruct them to dial 911. Give tasks to others. With more hands, you'll be able to do more, and it helps everyone feel better since they have something they can do to assist. It also eliminates the sense of powerlessness and fear.

- They will panic if they can see that you are panicking. They will remain quiet if you remain calm. Calm is preferable. Careful, exact, and thoughtful people are calm. Being calm will help others to be peaceful.

- Maintain and carry a mobile HAM radio, ideally one with increased power. Make sure you are familiar with the local emergency channels. Except for emergency communications, using a HAM radio requires a license. Understand the emergency frequency in your area. An analog radio may be your sole option for reaching emergency services if mobile phone towers go down if you are in an area with poor phone reception.

8.7 RECIPES

There are many different ways that your plants and essential oils may be used. Some of these date back a long time and have been in use for many years.

- **Essential Oils**

It's not the same as infused. When a plant is distilled, the water and oil are separated by converting the water into steam, and the oil is extracted. If you want to do things the hard way, you'll need a proper distillation apparatus, which is considerably more than you'll need unless you also want to make moonshine. Whatever plant you choose, place it in a saucepan or crockpot with water on top to create an essential oil. Not more than 3/4 of the way filled is ideal. Turn the pot's cover upside down and place it on top. This happens when steam condenses from the evaporation of water and drips into the pot from the top. When the water is hot enough to feel, simmer the mixture for 4 hours on low heat. Continue operating it until it is almost unrecognizable and totally cooked down. Remove it from the stove and leave it in your refrigerator or another cold location overnight. The water will have a very thin film of oil on top of it when you look at it the following day. Your essential oil is that. Skim it off and put it in a different, preferably dark-colored

container to keep the light out. Even if there is a little amount of water remaining, you may boil it off if you prefer. Be careful to keep items in a basement or another cold, dark location.

- **Infused Oils**

These are really simple to create and a crucial step in many herbal medicines.

Oil and herbs should be combined in a container at a ratio of 1:5. The most often used oils are olive, grapeseed, and coconut. However, any kind of edible oil will typically suffice. Make sure to combine and shake it.

Then, much as when making sun tea, all you are required to do is put it outdoors in the sunlight for approximately a month. The natural lipids in the oil will bond to the color, scent, and active components of the plant. The gradual approach is that. You may hasten the process by heating an oven to 300 °F, putting the jar inside, turning the oven off, and leaving the jar there for three hours. Alternatively, you may simmer it in a saucepan on the stovetop for about 30 minutes.

The oil should be strained and separated from the residual plant material before use. Squeeze it out completely since the last droplets are the finest. Don't be scared to prepare a large quantity to have on hand since these oils may last for approximately a year.

- **Lotion/ Cream**

Balms and salve are prepared quite similarly to lotions; however, the ratio makes a lotion considerably thinner. Make a lotion by following the same steps as for the balm but use 12 oz of beeswax and 34 cups of oil instead. There is one more stage to making a cream after melting and blending the oil/wax compound; blend the substance with a blender. Start it off slowly and add a small amount of water gradually. You want it to combine just enough to create a swirl in the middle, which may need some trying. Only then should you add the water as quickly as you can without creating a mess. Oil should emulsify when you add water, breaking up the fats into invisible droplets that are floating in the liquid. You'll be able to tell the mixture is functioning when it turns thick and creamy. Now is an excellent time to use up any essential oils you may have lying around, whether for medicinal purposes or just to enhance the aroma.

- **Salves and balms**

These items are made by combining beeswax with herb-infused oil. Salves and balms are almost identical, with the exception that balms are thicker and more portable since they include more beeswax. You must first have an infused oil, as we discussed before, in order to produce a balm or salve. Combine your oil or oils with 1.5oz of beeswax in a jar and store in a cool, dark place for up to three months for the best results. Put the jar into the pot and heat it up with an inch of water. Set the heat to a medium setting. Continue stirring as it heats. When everything has melted and combined, the heat may be turned off. You may put the oil/wax combination in a tin similar to the one used for lip balms. The waxy disc will harden as it cools, making it simple to apply with a dab of your fingertips and a little massage.

- **Tincture**

An herbal extract that has been dissolved in ethanol is a tincture (aka ethyl alcohol). Less than 20% alcohol should make up the whole solution. Vinegar and alcohol are also acceptable alternatives. Though they won't last, they should be prepared as needed. The herb eventually becomes less potent as a result of the alcohol and vinegar's tendency to "denature" it over time. This is a good method for creating a liquid, concentrated form of the plant for consumption.

- **Poultice**

Sores and cuts may be soothed with this soft mass of wet, crushed herbs distributed on a towel and then placed on the wound's surface. However, they are not always hot. The first step in making a poultice is to slice the plant into small pieces and then mix or ground it into a paste. Adding a little amount of water at a time will probably be necessary throughout this procedure.

It's done when it's a thick ooze. Towels or textiles may be treated with this goo. To prevent the herbal paste from spilling out, fold the fabric several times at the edges; nevertheless, the liquid must begin to leak through. What we desire is that. Depending on your requirements, you may either prepare them in advance to keep in plastic bags and freeze or simply use them straight away. A warmed or chilled poultice may be applied to the affected area to minimize swelling. A bandage or other covering should be used to secure the poultice cloth to the afflicted area in either case. These may be changed out every day.

Chapter 9:

PREPPER'S WATER

Finding a clean water source is your first concern, whether you are lost in the wilderness or are dealing with an emergency. Although food and shelter are essential for existence, water is considerably more crucial. Your organs will shut down if you go without water for more than three days while engaging in continual physical activity. The average person needs roughly two liters of water every day to sustain their metabolism, digestion, blood circulation, and temperature regulation, among other bodily functions.

Finding a water source in the wilderness is not the only issue. Even rushing water from lakes, rivers, or streams cannot be consumed in its natural state. You must first learn how to purify the water to ensure that it is safe to consume. In the best-case scenario, you will have the equipment and instruments needed to purify your water, but sometimes that won't be possible in the wild. There are methods for obtaining water and purifying it using items found outside to make it as safe as possible. This chapter will cover how to locate water in the wilderness, how to filter and store it, and exactly how to properly dispose of waste outside.

9.1 HOW DO YOU LOCATE SOURCES OF WATER?

To be on the safe side, look for moving water, as bacteria are less likely to develop in a fluid environment. Small streams and rivers are your best bet, but larger bodies of water tend to be polluted upstream. Water bodies like lakes and ponds, if properly filtered and purified, provide an additional alternative since stagnation promotes bacterial development.

If you're looking for nearby bodies of water, the first thing you need to do is pay attention to your surroundings. Even from a great distance, you'll be able to hear the rushing stream. Animal tracks in the dirt might lead you to a water source, so be on the lookout. Wildlife knows it needs water to survive and hence stays close by. Watch out for areas that are crawling with insects due to the presence of water since they will eventually lead you to a nearby stream.

There are water sources even in the most remote locations if you look for animal prints in the sand and birds in the sky. It's also a good idea to move to lower land, like valleys and ditches, since water flows downhill.

As an alternative method, you may collect rainwater, which has the lowest chance of causing bacterial infection in any water source that you can consume outdoors. Take into consideration that this only applies to areas outside of cities, where pollution tends to be higher. Rainwater would be polluted by all the contaminants in the air before you collect it. Thus, you should avoid collecting it at all costs.

Set up whatever containers you have on hand to collect rainwater. Most containers you carry in the bush are not wide enough to hold enough rainwater; thus, this may not be the most reliable method. For a larger containment area, attach a tarp or water-resistant cloth to each corner of a tree and place some weight in the center. The volume of water you will be able to collect in a short period of time will be substantial. Your tarp may be used to fill up any container you have by tilting it a little bit but do it carefully to prevent squandering the water you've collected inside of it. There are other methods, like collecting heavy morning dew off plants, that may keep you hydrated until you can locate a reliable water source. Just go on a stroll in the thick grass just before sunrise, tie a t-shirt around your waist, or tuck it in your pocket. Plants produce a lot of drinkable dew in the early morning due to atmospheric conditions. In order to remove excess water from the garment, you may either wring it out carefully in a water bottle or just suck it up with your mouth. Plant leaves may be collected by tying a plastic bag over them in the early morning. Throughout the day, plant roots gather water from the soil, which travels up toward the leaves and evaporates when exposed to the light. It is possible to collect water before it evaporates by wrapping a plastic bag around a branch. Collecting water is made simpler by placing a heavy object in the bag, such as a boulder.

In addition to fruits and vegetables, there are other plant-based water sources. In the desert, plant roots and even cactus plants may be used to get water. Collect a few of these plants in a container and break them with a heavy rock to get the water out. There will be some liquid in the resulting pulp, which may keep you going for a while until you can find a better source of water. Of course, this method can only be used in areas like tropical forests, where it has a high probability of success. Coconuts are the best source of fat in these forested areas. Drinking the water from ripe coconuts may cause diarrhea, upset your stomach, and cause even more dehydration, so go for the freshest ones.

You may also search for water in rock crevices and tree crotches. In an emergency, they may be useful even if they don't provide much water. Birds may lead you to these locations since they are skilled at spotting minute water sources. To collect the water, use a piece of cloth in the same way you would for collecting dew in the morning. Creating an underground still is a more serious way to locate a water source and ensure that there is always enough water on hand. If you are unable to dig a hole, you may create a still above ground, but this will not provide you with the same quantity of water. Tools such as a container, pebbles, a plastic sheet, straw or a long tube, and a shovel will be needed for this method.

The first step is to choose a location that receives the maximum sunlight. Then, make a hole large enough to accommodate your containment device. Put one end of the tubing in the container and the other end on the ground so that the collected water may be drunk from the tubing itself.

If you're unable to make a tube using the materials you have at hand, you may simply refill the container and place it back in the hole. To keep the plastic sheet in place, place heavy boulders on the ends and place them over the hole. To create a dripping effect, place a smaller rock in the middle and let the water fall into the container below.

During the day, the sun's heat causes the groundwater to condense, which is how the system works. If the plastic sheet is filled with water, it will rise upward and be collected at the bottom of the container. When the reservoir is full, water will flow into the container on its own. This method can provide you with up to one liter of drinkable water every day, so you might need to make a few more stills to collect enough.

If you're stranded in a snowy area, melting the snow or ice around you makes it much easier to collect water. If you eat snow directly, you'll get dehydrated; thus, you should avoid it at all costs. To ensure that it is safe to eat, it must first be purified. The best way to enjoy it is to combine it with some water since it might develop an unpleasant taste when eaten on its own.

9.2 CONDENSATION

Water may also be extracted by condensation. Condensation is a fantastic technique to use in all environments, including the desert. Using heat (such as from a fire or the sun) and an object made of glass, plastic, or metal, you may use the process of condensation to turn liquid, moisture, and water vapor in the air into water that can be consumed. This can be done to produce drinkable water.

9.2.1 METHOD FOR SOLAR STILL CONDENSATION

- Find a wet area that spends most of the day exposed to sunlight.
- Dig a bowl-shaped hole that is approximately 2 inches deep and 3 feet wide, as well as a smooth sump suitable for your container (such as a leaf, plastic bag, metal can, etc.) in the center of the bowl. Place your container in the middle, at the lowest position, after that.
- Cover the hole with plastic, followed by filling the holes' sides with rock and dirt.
- Put a stone in the center of the plastic, tarp, or canvas over the container that collects the condensation. Allow the material to droop for about 12 inches so that it may be shaped into an inverted cone. Next, fill the edges of the material with earth to further secure it.
- The earth will get heated by the sun, releasing moisture that eventually condenses on the plastic cover. The condensation will drop into the container holding your water supply after flowing to the lowest point, which is the rock.

9.2.2 TREE LIMB CONDENSATION METHOD WITH A BAG AROUND IT (TRANSPIRATION):

- Cut a hole the size of a dime in the bottom corner of a plastic bag to allow water to escape.
- Find a tree limb that is easily accessible and covered with leaves.
- With the bottom hole of the plastic bag secured over the branch of leaves, zip-tie it in place.
- To stock your supply, place a container just below the hole in the bag and let the water drip for a day.

9.3 HOW TO MAKE WATER PURE?

Here are various methods for removing contaminants, germs, and parasites from water in the wild:

- **Boiling**

Boiling water is the quickest and most straightforward method of purification, assuming you have the necessary tools and a bonfire or stove. A pot of boiling water should contain rolling bubbles for at least 5 minutes before you may remove it from the heat. To avoid burning your lips and tongue, wait until it has cooled before drinking.

- **Purification pumps**

If you visit a shop that sells camping and outdoor gear, you'll definitely discover a wide variety of pumps with purifiers and filters to ensure that only drinking water exits directly into your bottle of water. This is accomplished by chemically modifying water after it has been squeezed through a ceramic or charcoal filter.

The purifying process occurs while you suck water straight into your mouth with certain high-tech water bottles; you aren't required to pump the water into a different bottle.

- **Purification pills and drops**

Adding a few purification drops or pills to wild water is a quick, low-cost, although maybe not the best-tasting way to clean it up. Iodine is the most often utilized chemical; however, potassium permanganate or chlorine are also useful. Before drinking, let the water be treated with chemicals for at least twenty minutes. You may also combine the water with powdered mixtures to cover up any flavor.

- **Create a ground evaporation trap**

All of the above ways need carrying water or having a water source nearby, but what if there is none? NatureSkills.com says you can get water out of the ground by digging a pit and putting a container at the bottom. Put plastic over the hole to prevent moisture evaporation, and place a light object (a rock, maybe) in the middle of the cover to create a dip. Water drops into the container as it drips onto the lid after condensing there as it evaporates from the bottom up.

Just try to remember to carry some, as this final technique isn't the quickest way to acquire drinkable water. Be prepared with this procedure and a container with a plastic cover in case of an emergency, though.

9.4 MAKING A WATER CONTAINMENT DEVICE?

In the best-case scenario, you will carry a water container to store your water while you are out in nature. However, let's assume that you lack a container. You need to come up with another method for creating a water container from materials you may find around.

- **Wood container**

You may make the simplest kind of container out of wood. Find a dry wood or branch that is large enough to serve as a hollow water container. Since it is simpler to carve a bowl-shaped hole in an even flat surface, it is best to have a cutting instrument that can slice it in half lengthwise. Pick a healthy-looking log that doesn't have any rotten or cracked pieces.

The next step is to create a campfire and let it burn until the wood becomes quite hot. So that you may safely transport the coal, try to make some homemade thongs out of a split stick. Take a few coal pieces and place them on the log's smooth surface. Then, begin blowing on the coals to maintain their flame until they burn a hole in the wood. Continue until it forms a large enough hole to accommodate water. To remove the splinters and smooth out the waves, use a knife or a rock found nearby. To create your water container, repeat the process as much as you can.

- **Birch bark**

If you happen to come upon a birch tree in the area, another suggestion is to use the bark. Use a survival knife or chisel to chop off and peel bark if you have one. In order to make it simpler for you to shape a rectangular piece into a water container, try to cut the piece as accurately as you are able to. Next, in order to make the bark flexible enough to fold and shape, you will need to use heat from a campfire. The concept is to fold the corners into tiny triangular shapes before folding them once more to the sides to create a hollow, rectangular bowl for holding water. If you want to stop the bark from unfolding, you'll need to secure the sides with some kind of clip. By cutting a tiny stick lengthwise, halfway, or less in the middle, you may make a clip. The folded portions of the bark may be held with only two pieces, preventing them from unfolding once again. If you see a bamboo stalk, cut it to create a sealing junction and use it to make a cup.

- **Animal skins**

Animal skins may also be used to make a water container. Take the stomach of any large animal and wash it many times in water to do this. You must boil some water, remove it from the heat, and then soak the stomach for two hours. The procedure should be repeated as often as possible until the soaking water becomes clear after the stomach has been left in it. The stomach should next be penetrated to scrape the insides, but you must be careful not to puncture it. To make the scraping easier, it is best to perform this while the stomach is warm. Once you're finished, re-soak the stomach for 30 minutes in some boiling water. Tie one end of the stomach to the other to form a pouch to hold water and seal the top.

- **Plant parts**

Other plant components, such as coconut shells, may be used to make water bottles, but you must carve a little cork from a short branch to seal the opening. To leave the shell empty and prevent the fruit from rotting, you must remove all the inside components. Remove any splinters by smoothing off the outside wooden portion.

9.5 OUTDOOR DISPOSAL OF WASTE

You must learn how to properly dispose of waste in the wilderness. Similar to animal feces, human feces are full of germs and must be properly buried to prevent contamination. Additionally, there are guidelines about how to urinate in the wild.

You must first choose a location distant from a route that other campers and hikers use.

To find a place to pee, it's a decent rule of thumb to count 70 steps from the nearest path. Use a location behind a tree, a shrub, or a rock. To prevent wetting your clothing or boots, you must aim correctly. Avoid urinating in lakes, ponds, or other small bodies of water to prevent pollution. In order to better aim if you don't want to take off your clothes, some women use a pee funnel. This is a safer choice since many women risk contracting poison ivy while using the restroom outside.

There are two alternatives for defecation: bury the waste or pack it until you can safely dispose of it. While it would seem more sensible to bury your waste, certain places do not allow it. There are four considerations you must make before properly disposing of your waste.

- You must be careful not to contaminate any water sources.
- Make sure nobody else comes into contact with your waste.
- Make sure to minimize your risk of spreading diseases.
- You must bury your waste in a location where it can decompose properly.

9.5.1 CONSTRUCTING A CATHOLE

Cat hole digging is the method used most often. The safest thing to do in outdoors is to maximize decomposition, which encourages plant development. You must locate a location with organic soil. For this purpose, you should include a little trowel with your equipment. Start by walking 70 steps away from hiking trails and waterways to choose a location with usable soil. At the very least, the hole should be 6 inches deep and 4 inches wide. When you're finished, fill the hole with dirt from the surrounding area. To prevent contamination, make sure your trowel does not come into contact with your feces.

9.5.2 BUILD A BATHROOM

You may dig a hole after you're finished if it is urgent and you didn't have time to do it before. If you don't have a trowel, you may use a stick to move your waste into the hole and cover it. Digging a toilet is a different alternative. When camping over a longer period with a small group of people, this option is used. You must dig a trench that is the same size as a cat hole but longer. To identify which holes have been filled, you might mark the ends with a rock or stick. Each hole should, of course, be covered as quickly as it is filled with trash. Latrines should not be used often since they are not the best choice in terms of natural decomposition.

9.5.3 Utilizing toilet paper or leaves

Even if carrying toilet paper may not be feasible, if you can, avoid throwing away wet wipes or other feminine hygiene items on the ground. Although you may buy "green" toilet paper that will decompose swiftly, they don't decompose quickly. While certain locations allow for the burial of unattended toilet paper, it may still take up to a year for the material to decompose properly. Use them as a very last option. Make sure to bury it deep in the kitty hole if you decide to do this. If you don't have toilet paper, you may wipe with leaves, smooth pebbles you can find in waterways, and packed snow.

9.5.4 Prior to safely disposing of it, place your trash in a bag

The alternative is to place your trash in a bag until you can dispose of it safely. Most hikers and mountain climbers follow this practice in order to protect the environment. Bring a Waste Alleviation and Gelling (WAG) bag if you select for packing. The WAG bag is made out of an outer bag that may be sealed and an inside bag for your intimates. Outside, there are crystals that transform your waste into a gel, turning it into an inert substance. Once you're through, just seal the outer bag after removing the air from the inside and carry the bag until you can properly dispose of it. After that, fold the inside bag in half.

Avoiding panic is the most crucial thing. It's best to be prepared before going on a camping vacation, of course. But if you don't have the right equipment, we hope you can use the advice in this chapter to learn how to get water from various sources in the wilderness, how to purify it, and how to take it with you. To prevent contamination, it's also crucial to keep in mind the proper waste disposal techniques.

Chapter 10:

PREPPER'S FOOD

Food is the third most crucial resource in a survival scenario, behind water and shelter. There is a limit to how long you can go without eating. You will need some kind of food production if you want to live off the grid indefinitely. As we have seen in several scenarios, including earthquakes, tornadoes, and even the recent pandemic, the disruption of local and international transportation routes has a significant influence on the availability of food. Going to the local grocery store may not be an option, and even if it is, it is not a long-term answer if you are in a survival crisis.

Because your safety is crucial, you should avoid attracting potential predators. A big draw for the predatory game is food. Avoid leaving any traces of foodstuff at your campsites, such as crumbs or leftovers, to protect your food and yourself from encountering predators drawn to food. It is also a good idea to store your food nearby, such as in a tree, and away from your campsite.

In the event of a global disease or natural catastrophe, learning how to store your food might save you both time and money. To begin stockpiling food in case of an emergency, follow the procedures outlined in this chapter.

1. Analyze The Capacity Of Your Food Storage

Shelf-stable, the safest place for non-perishable food, is at room temperature, away from sudden changes in temperature. They need to be protected from pests and always kept dry.

A. What's the Best Place to Store Your Food Reserves?

In unfinished basements and attics, food should not be kept, particularly if the temperature is not controlled. Check out locations that are out of the way yet still meet all your food storage needs.

Which of the cabinets or shelves in your kitchenette or wardrobe are empty? What kind of storage container do you have that's big enough to hold your stockpile? To preserve the food out of harm's way, do you have adequate space? Does your living room have a location to keep the food?

B. Decide on a Storage Location

You'll need to pick a site for your stockpile after considering things like water, temperature, and accessibility. If you don't record your measurements, you'll forget how much room you have to work with. While out and about, take a photo of the place and save it on your phone for future reference.

2. Determine How Much Food To Store

Preparation is key when it comes to storing food in case of an emergency. By storing food, you won't waste money and resources.

A. Learn about the dietary habits of your family

Prior to determining your calorie needs, you must first figure out how much food everyone eats on a typical day. Additionally, you need to monitor the everyday meals that your family eats.

- Make a list of the snacks, daily meals, desserts, and drinks that each of the family members typically consumes. Create a list of the quantity and specific items.

- List any dietary restrictions you may have.

- You consider their needs as well when others, like grandparents, could use your house as a safe haven in an emergency.

- Replace perishable items on your shopping lists with non-perishable ones, such as boxed milk, in favor of cold milk.

- If a suitable non-perishable substitute is not available, cross that item off your list.

B. Carry out the calculations

The US Department of Homeland Security publishes data on food supplies at Ready.gov. They advise having enough non-perishable food on hand to feed one household for three days. A 2-week stockpile is advised by the FEMA and Red Cross.

- Make a list of the exact meals and drinks that each member of the family eats during the day, along with the necessary non-perishable substitutes.

- Indicate how many servings of each item on your list are eaten each day.

- For a three-day supply, multiply each serving size by 3, then note the result. That person needs that many portions of each item for a 3-day supply.

- For the 2-week supply, multiply by 14 rather than 3 to get the answer.

- For every family member, repeat the procedure.

- Create a new list of all the foods you like to eat. The serving size that a family will need is calculated by adding the servings of each person who eats the same meal throughout the day.

- If you want to know how many servings of a certain product seem to be included in one container, look at the serving size information that is shown above the can, box, or jar.

- Keep in mind that your data represents the number of servings, not the number of cans or jars that is necessary.

To get the desired number of servings, you must calculate how many containers are necessary.

C. Increasing Your Stockpile: How to Do It

The number of daily servings your complete family need may be calculated by dividing the totals on the master list by three. If you intend on stockpiling for a certain number of days, double this amount by that number. The total number of servings of peanut butter the family will consume over the course of a month is 90; thus, multiplying 30 by 3 will give you the total number of peanut butter servings your family will consume in a month.

3. <u>Decide Which Food To Keep</u>

To save space, you don't need to save everything your family consumes over the course of a day or three.

A. Decide what you and your family need

Determine which items on your grocery list are most healthful and which are really necessary. If you've got the space, you should stockpile these items.

- Something with a large amount of salt will make you thirsty, and you'll be unable to drink much of anything as a result.
- Choose one "desirable" object for each member of the family to boost spirits during a crisis.
- Non-perishable foods should be stored in jars, canned goods, or sealed containers.
- Everyone should drink at least one gallon of water each day, according to the US Public Health Association.

B. The Foods You Must Store in Your Stockpile

Most foods don't need to be cooked and may be kept for up to two years in the refrigerator. Cans are the best way to keep meats and vegetables fresh for a lengthy period.

- Jelly
- White rice
- Dried fruit
- Dry cereal
- Bottled water
- Peanut butter
- Canned pasta
- Unsalted nuts
- Protein bars and granola bars
- Canned beef
- Boxed or canned milk

C. Foods You Should Store in Your Stockpile

Just a handful of "luxury" food items in your stockpile may help families deal with stress and retain a positive mindset in the event of an emergency.

- Fruit juice

- Fruit snacks
- Hard candy
- Unique crackers
- Mix for instant cocoa
- Combination of instant tea
- Cookies mix for instant coffee
- Drink mixes made with powder

4. Purchase A Few Items At Once

It's not necessary to purchase all of your supplies at once while building an emergency food supply. Many establishments impose restrictions on how many essential items you may purchase in a single visit, particularly if a pandemic has already started in nearby areas. It's essential to start hoarding as a result, especially if there is no immediate need. Every time you go to the grocery store, buy no more than two or three items. This saves you money and helps the environment.

5. Prepare Your Food Supplies

As you amass products, store them in an assigned storage area in an organized manner. To guarantee that items are used first, those with the earliest expiry dates must be put at the front or top of the pile. The simplest way to organize goods is to keep everything all together into a list of "use by" dates, starting with the earliest and ending with the latest.

A. What Are the Benefits of Preparing an Emergency Food Supply?

Shelter-in-place orders, worldwide pandemic quarantines, emergency state declarations, and natural calamities aren't frequent, but they're possible. For a variety of reasons, you may not be able to go shopping; shops may be unable to get sufficient goods; or, in the case of a power outage, your refrigerator may be rendered useless. Preparing for these disasters, even if you won't receive an advance warning, can help you.

B. Stockpiling Is A Success!

An emergency food stockpile must always be maintained. The time it takes to build up a stockpile might be days, weeks, or even months. When you make this, you'll have to inspect it every six months to make sure there are no expired or ruined goods. Check that your emergency food supply contains at least one manual can opener, as well as a few utensils.

10.2 HOW TO PRODUCE FOOD ON YOUR OWN

You may begin by growing your own vegetables and fruit to provide a long-term food source for yourself and your family. So many different types of things could be grown that you could almost entirely subsist on them. Your farmland may just be used for farming, or it may be a source of income if your operations are expanded. The yield is sometimes so large that people are forced to share their produce with others or risk it spoiling, even if they are cultivating on a little plot of land. As an example, if you plant lettuce in your garden, you may expect to harvest a lot of it. You can easily sell or give away this kind of vegetable since it doesn't have a lengthy shelf life, and there aren't any excellent techniques to preserve it. You may also grow your own fruits and vegetables using organic methods, which will provide higher-quality fruits and vegetables that can be sold at a higher price. To begin producing your own food, let's take a look at a few of the fundamentals.

10.3 THE FUNDAMENTALS OF FERTILIZING THE SOIL

Good soil serves as a sort of warehouse for anything that plants require to thrive. It also serves as a comfortable base for the plant to develop roots that support development aboveground. It includes nutrients, air, water, and organic matter. Your garden soil can be ready for use straight away, depending on where you are and the local weather. To get the soil in excellent shape, however, you could need to do extensive repair work, or you might need to add whole new soil to the area to make it suitable for growing plants.

Make sure the soil is in excellent shape if you want to rely on it over the long term. If not, you may be unable to benefit from it beyond the first harvest. The foundation of successful farming is high-quality soil that has been properly maintained and can provide you with an endless supply of food. Begin by learning more about the soil in your area before getting started with planting or searching for plants.

Different soil types exist in various regions, and these variations will have an influence on the kind of fruits and vegetables you may plant and how well they will thrive. You should invest in having enough dirt dumped if you don't already have the correct soil.

Due to the amount of clay in the sea, certain regions may have very wet and oily soil, whilst other regions may have stony soil with very little fine-grained material. Additionally, certain areas have very fine dirt that, when dried, produces clumps that are hard and solid. In theory, you want soil that is easily crumbled, black, can contain a lot of moisture, is free of pebbles, and won't solidify.

You may use a variety of items to create your own organic soil and a variety of items to aid in the better growth of your crops. You do have the choice to buy pre-packaged organic material, but you can only store so much before it runs out or becomes worse. One excellent tip for getting things going well is to mix the organic matter with the soil while you are first placing it down. This significantly increases the soil's nutritional value, giving you a stronger foundation that will serve you for much longer in the future. Organic matter and natural compost help your soil retain more water and absorb nutrients. Compost, for example, is a fantastic source of energy for smaller microbes, which helps to drive the ecosystem. Simply piling up brown and green layers is a simple approach to creating your own organic material. Straw, cardboard, and dried leaves are examples of brown liners, whereas leftover food, livestock manure, and green grass are examples of green liners. All you have to do to help it break down more quickly and evenly is make sure it's wet and keep rotating it often.

To help your crops, you may also use a mixture of organic and synthetic mulch. Grass clippings, shredded bark, hay, sawdust, and other types of natural waste materials are examples of organic mulch. Mulch is laid over the agricultural field to reduce evaporation and protect it from extreme weather conditions. Additionally, it may considerably slow down weed growth and reduce the amount of unsustainable pest infestation. This organic mulch helps the ground underneath it retains water better and provides it with a variety of nutrients and minerals as it gently breaks down. Small pebbles, gravel, landscape fabric, or even plastic sheets may be used as inorganic mulch. Artificial mulches provide some of the same protective benefits as natural mulch, but they don't contribute any extra nutrients. More significantly, you don't need to replace these mulches every year, and you may reuse a sheet of plastic for a number of years. However, if you want to improve the soil's quality, they are great.

Additionally, you have the choice to use fertilizer to aid in your crops' development. Everything from liquid or dry pesticides to synthetic or natural pesticides will fall under this category. In general, natural fertilizers will release their nutrients more gradually but for a longer period than commercial fertilizers, which will operate quickly but only temporarily. Additionally, natural fertilizers won't have any side effects, but artificial ones always run the danger of wiping out the microorganisms that support the growth of your crops.

10.4 GROWING A SURVIVAL GARDEN

Start with the basics and go from there. After that, drop all pretenses. You won't master the art of survival gardening overnight. Making it all work requires many seasons of gardening expertise, foraging skills, understanding of seed storage and tree multiplication, as well as a good dose of luck. But you have to begin somewhere. No matter how large or tiny in the garden. As your abilities advance, you may expand the narrative until it meets all your needs for survival. If you are just starting off homesteading and becoming closer to nature, everything will take some practice.

- Choosing seeds
- Planting seeds
- Keeping seeds
- Cultivated herbs
- Preparing the garden's design
- Harvesting when it is appropriate
- Preserving and canning
- Animal rearing
- Composting
- Vermicomposting

Avoid being discouraged by the amount of effort or knowledge that's necessary since the pride of self-sufficiency that comes from producing healthy food for your entire family will be well worth it! And that fact alone has the ability to completely transform the way you perceive food, the production of food throughout the world, and the best ways to maintain your health in an environment that is always shifting and becoming more challenging.

When designing your yard, think about including plants that can tolerate both full sun and partial shade. Take advantage of the variety in your garden to ensure that you are getting all the essential nutrients you need each day.

The following crops should be included in your preparedness garden if you want to live off the grid:

- Corn
- Beans
- Onions
- Carrots
- Squash
- Potatoes
- Tomatoes

To grow a strong survival garden, you need a firm base of soil. To help you get started, we've compiled a list of helpful hints and techniques.

10.4.1 WATERING

When it comes to your survival garden's potential to generate significant amounts of food, you need to water it. It is possible to get irrigation water from a river, lake, or spring. Installing a water pump is an expensive proposition; instead, look into free or low-cost sources of natural water.

10.4.2 COMPOST

The idea that composting is overly labor-intensive, smelly, and dirty is among the most widespread misunderstandings about it. Although these comments may be true if you compost incorrectly, the process of composting is really pretty easy and straightforward. Wait for your combination to transform into humus (the finest soil enhancer on the market!) after layering organic components and adding a little amount of soil and water. Afterward, you may use this compost to enrich your garden soil, fertilize the grass, feed your growing plants, and more. Once you get your compost pile up and running, you will discover that it is a simple and straightforward method to convert organic waste, such as food scraps and other organic materials, into a substance that is helpful to your plants.

A. Composting Methods

You should be aware that there are two types of composting: cold composting and hot composting. Gather yard waste or organic materials from your garbage, such as fruit and vegetable peels, eggshells, coffee grounds, and filters, and arrange them in a container to start cold composting. The material will deteriorate within a year. Hot composting requires more effort from you, but it yields results more quickly; in warm weather, compost will be ready in 1-3 months. Nitrogen, oxygen, carbon, and water are the four ingredients needed for hot compost that cooks quickly.

The breakdown process is accelerated when such components are combined because microbes are fed. You may make a large batch of compost in the spring or autumn when there is a bunch of general waste, then start another batch while the first one "cooks." Worms are used in the creation of vermicompost. These worms produce castings that are rich in nitrogen when they consume your food leftovers. But you can't simply employ any worms for this; Redworms are required to exist. Composting worms may be purchased at a fair price either online or at garden supply stores. Either option is viable.

B. __What To Compost__

Composting is a great method to recycle goods in your fridge that have beyond their sell-by date, decreasing food waste. Instead of being tossed, certain forms of yard waste can be composted. To get your compost pile started, gather the following ingredients.:

- Straw
- Eggshells
- Fruit scraps
- Dry leaves
- Coffee grounds
- Vegetable scraps
- Newspaper shredded
- Chips of wood and bark
- Untreated wood's sawdust
- Clippings from plants and grass

Composting may be as simple as keeping a container inside your kitchen to collect waste while you cook. Making your own outdoor or indoor compost bin is an excellent alternative to buying one. Frozen kitchen scraps are another option for holding perishables once you're prepared to add them to the bigger outdoor pile.

C. Making Hot Compost

Wait until you've created a pile of items that is three feet high before starting your own heated compost heap. You should combine your green and wet goods with your dry and brown ones. Brown materials include wood shavings that are high in carbon, shredded tree branches, cardboard, straw or hay, newspaper, and dried plant debris. Green resources, which all include nitrogen, include coffee grounds, grass trimmings, fresh plants, animal manures (but not from cats or dogs), and animal waste from the kitchen. For the greatest results, start by dividing the items inside your compost pile into three parts brown and one part green. Add additional brown materials and aerate your compost pile more often if it looks to be very wet and smelly.

Hydrate it with water and greens if it seems too brown and dried.

- Spritz your pile.
- Move your pile.
- Give your garden food.

10.4.3 GARDENING FOR SURVIVAL AND PROTECTION

If your survival garden is the sole source of food for your family, you must protect and preserve it. If anything happens to your crop, it might put the well-being of your family's diet at risk. Use the following tactics to safeguard your survival garden:

- Fences
- Ditches
- Barbed wire

10.5 FINDING FOOD IN THE WILDERNESS?

You have many choices. You are right if you think of a Paleolithic guy. Food was obtained by hunting or foraging before farms were established by humans. The default choices are these:

10.5.1 HUNTING

In addition to protection, guns are also useful for obtaining food. One cartridge of ammunition and some hunting time can get you 45-75 pounds of flesh from a deer. 6.5 Creedmoor ammunition from a good manufacturer costs roughly $2.40. Return on investment was satisfactory. Even better, if you're a skilled archer, you can get the missile back and utilize it once more.

Many people don't have easy access to firearms. Do what you can if you're able to. In the next chapter, we'll go into further detail on firearm safety and usage. It's not simple to go hunting. Go out with someone who has done it before if you never have. Depending on the kind of animal you choose to hunt, there is plenty to learn. A rifle may be necessary to protect oneself from wild animals like mountain lions or brown bears. If a wild predator is very hungry, or if they believe that you are a danger to their young, they might attack you.

The protein in game animals is great. Prey animals, such as rabbits, deer, and others, have very little fat, which is a major disadvantage. Many of us were told as children that eating animal fat was harmful to our health. Those claims are bogus. Animal fat is an excellent source of fat for humans. A bear is an excellent choice for fatty meals.

10.5.2 FISHING

Many individuals dislike eating fish. If you find yourself in a difficult situation, you must overcome it. Every day, 125 million people in Japan consume fish. In the absence of allergies, of course, you'll be OK. Fish is a terrific source of protein, and fishing can be done casually, which is one of its many benefits.

It is easy to construct a V-shaped rock wall in a shallow river or stream. You're not building a dam. You are building a fence with openings that are small enough for water to readily flow through but not for fish. This barrier holds the fish in place, so you may approach them at your convenience and catch them with a net or a spear.

Spearfishing is a fantastic alternative if you're in the ocean's shallows, particularly around reefs and sandbars. Wood may be used to create a spear with a dozen pointed sticks affixed to the end that is placed in various orientations to resemble porcupine quills. This allows you to approach fish extremely closely if you're patient and motionless. For streams, you may lay up fishing lines with bait and hooks along the water's edge, wait until one of them begins to move, and then reel it in. You have a higher chance of catching a fish if you have more hooks out there. Running a rope between two points while securing both ends to trees is one simple approach. The bait and hooks should then dangle just above the water's surface after you have tied and handed a few lines down the rope.

The fish will come to you if you have or create nets that you may place up along a river.

Whatever way you use, be careful to remove everything you've put up. By trapping and collecting more fish than is required, we don't want to entirely upset the ecology.

The ideal fishing scenario is one in which the fish are caught by themselves. The better off you are with fewer jobs to do. Laziness is not an issue here. This is about making the most of your time to do as much as possible. If you can capture fish, wouldn't it be better if you could also distill water, make improvements to your shelter, or take care of a garden at the same time?

10.5.3 TRAPPING

To find out what you can and cannot do with reference to trapping, check your local regulations just as you would for hunting and fishing. Do what you choose if conditions deteriorate to the point that laws are nullified. In that, you may set up a vast trap network and visit them a few times each day, and trapping is similar to fishing. It is an extremely cheap and low-energy method of gathering wild meat. We are mostly discussing rabbits, squirrels, and maybe beavers. Although they aren't normally your first pick, they are absolutely edible and taste fantastic in stews.

If you own a garden, setting a trap there will accomplish two goals at once; it will safeguard your veggies, and it will allow you to catch a bunny for breakfast.

Snares are similarly effective but far more challenging and unreliable. The most effective squirrel-trapping method I've seen is to lean a limb onto a tree at an angle of 90°. Make a slipknot at the business end of the snare, about an inch away from the branch, and tie it along the branch. Like all other organisms, squirrels are sluggish. It is easier to climb a tree's 90-degree branch than it is a 180-degree trunk. If you're fortunate, a squirrel will accidentally tighten your slipknot by running headlong into it. If you build it correctly and are a bit fortunate, a dozen of these snares may catch one squirrel each day.

The large leg traps made from metals that have the appearance of metal jaws are illegal, almost rare to buy except in antique shops, and very hazardous to use in any setting.

10.5.4 FORAGING

A field guide will certainly come in handy if you wish to go foraging. Where you reside has a significant impact on the guide you choose to utilize. It is essential to have a guide that is appropriate for your natural area since various plants grow in different places.

Although foraging is a fantastic approach to getting extra nourishment from plant sources, it is insufficient on its own. Eat no mushrooms. In any case, mushrooms don't have much nutritious value. Simply put, the risk is not worth it. Never consume wild mushrooms.

10.5.5 SCAVENGING

Roadkill may be consumed. It's logical that many individuals could find it unpleasant.

Numerous deer are killed by vehicles. The most recent estimate I could locate was from the USA in 2012. There were 1.2 million car accidents caused by striking deer. Between 1 and 6 out of every 100 auto accidents include animals. It's quite typical.

You probably know this if you reside in a region where they are widespread. Approximately 200 Americans die annually as a result of deer crashes. When you reside near them, they often begin to seem more like enormous pests than they do as lovely and magnificent creatures.

Nobody wants to eat roadkill. Not fillet mignon at all. However, an already-dead animal that is lying there for you to seize in a survival scenario might be a blessing.

To be safe for consumption, deceased animals must have expired only recently. In warm climes, meat degrades rapidly, and if you wish to eat it, you can bet that other animals, such as birds, insects, mice, and other creatures, want to as well. They may already have begun.

If you personally shoot the deer, you may be certain that it is as fresh as it gets.

You can immediately determine the animal's health by taking a glance at it. It is usually okay to consume if there aren't any open sores or splattering. It is dangerous if a dead deer has ruptures, exposed guts, or insects crawling all over it. The lifetime of a naturally frozen deer will be significantly increased since animals slaughtered in the winter are naturally chilled, and many of the creatures that would normally devour them are still hibernating. Simply avoid the area if there have been fly nests, maggots, or something else that makes you instinctively gag. Bad meat is very harmful; therefore, you should avoid eating it. Just follow your senses if anything seems strange, smells off, or looks off.

Chapter 11:

FOOD CANNING FOR PREPPERS

After obtaining food, food preservation comes in second. We are used to meals having very long shelf lives in today's society since preservatives are often added. You can't just add calcium phosphate or sodium nitrite when you're in the process of collecting, hunting, and cultivating your own food—and to be honest, you don't even want to. Better methods exist without the need for further processing or chemical additions.

For thousands of years, people have developed methods for preserving food and extending their lives. Famine and feast cycles were the only means of survival for humans before agriculture was invented. You had to collect much more food than you required during the harvesting season and then attempt to store it for the entire winter.

Keeping the food fresh for the sailors was important since seafarers had to handle dozens or even hundreds of people aboard a boat for lengthy trips without replenishment. Look at how people survived on transatlantic journeys between the 16th & 19th centuries to see how seriously individuals may prepare and ration.

11.1 BASICS OF CANNING: PRESERVATION AND DURATION

Meals may get rather monotonous in the thick of winter if you want to eat in season. On a stormy day, wouldn't it be lovely to go into your cupboard and take out a jar of peaches that are just right for summer? Food may be preserved by canning and kept in sealed containers that can be kept at room temperature.

It is possible to sterilize food that has been preserved in a jar by heating it via the process of canning. By boiling your food for a certain period of time and killing the hazardous microorganisms, proper canning procedures protect food from rotting. During the canning procedure, the air is forced out of the jar, and a vacuum is formed when the jar cools down and seals.

Here are two canning techniques:

1. **Water Bath**

This process, which is often referred to as "hot water canning," involves a large kettle of boiling water. Jars with contents are heated to 200 ° for a predetermined period while submerged in water. Process foods strong in acids, such as fruit, fruit-based goods, tomatoes, pickles, and pickled foods.

2. **Pressure Canning**

Pressure canning uses steam produced in a sealed compartment by a large kettle. The full jars in the kettle attain an internal temperature of 240 °F under a set pressure monitored by a dial gauge or weighted gauge on the pressure-canner lid. Utilize a pressure canner to preserve low-acid foods like beef, poultry, fish, as well as vegetables.

Be sure to consider your favorite seasonal meals while choosing what to can. Which do you like more in the summer, sun-kissed tomatoes or juicy strawberries? Pay attention to what is also cheap and plentiful. Unopened home canned goods have a one-year shelf life when kept in a cool, dry environment.

Two-year shelf life may be expected for handmade jams produced with sugar and canned in a heated water bath. For food safety, adhere to canning instructions.

- **Freezing Food**

Preparation, packaging, and freezing of food, while it is still fresh, is known as food freezing. It is essential that you freeze food as quickly as possible and at the proper freezing temperature to get the best results from freezing (0 degrees).

Freezer containers and freezer sheets keep food fresh for longer periods of time. Your food will be ruined if it comes into contact with the cold, dry air of the freezer. Even though freezer-damaged food is safe to eat, it has a bad taste.

To prevent freezer burn, here are three recommendations:

- To prevent food from being exposed to the air, be sure to wrap it tightly.
- Avoid temperature swings by keeping your freezer closed. Don't open the door until you know what you're taking.
- Your freezer's ventilation will be restricted, and damage to the freezer will be accelerated by overcrowding it.

- **Drying Food**

Among the earliest methods of food preservation, drying is still used today. When food is dried, a temperature that is both high enough to remove moisture and low enough to avoid frying is applied to it. Good air circulation aids in the consistent drying of the food. An electric dehydrator is a best and most effective way to dry or dehydrate food. In order to help with better temperature control, contemporary units are equipped with a thermostat and fan. Food may also be dried in an oven or in the sun, but the process is more time-consuming, and the results are less impressive than when using a dehydrator.

- **Using Spices**

It is common for Indians to utilize spices in their food. Preserving food with these spices is common practice. When it comes to food preservation, the use of simple spices and herbs is much superior to any other scientific method. Aside from flavoring and coloring food, spices are also used to keep it fresh and prevent spoilage. In addition to vinegar and alcohol, food preservation methods also involve the use of acidulants.

As an example, consider the following types of spices:

- **Black Pepper**

Because of its antifungal, antibacterial, and prebiotic properties, black pepper is an excellent flavoring for preserving food. Black pepper is essential to maintain the freshness of jams, pickles, preserves, and desserts. Peppercorns in pickles must be whole. Shelf life is extended by about a month if there is an opening in the preservation seal.

- **Salt**

Prior to refrigeration, salt was used to keep food fresh for many years. Meats, vegetables, and fish may all be preserved in this manner for an extended period. When food is salted, it removes moisture from the food. Because bacteria thrive in damp conditions, salting is an effective method of controlling the growth of microorganisms. When food was scarce, such as during the winter or drought, people would stockpile salt to urge them to eat more.

- **Ginger**

Ginger is a natural remedy for nausea, a flu-fighter, and a stimulant of salivation. As a food preservative, it's an excellent choice. The antibacterial and anti-carcinogenic properties of this spice make it ideal for long-term food preservation.

- **Cumin**

For many years, the seeds of cumin have been employed to preserve food. Parsley family member cumin is known as the Spice of the Ancients because of its tiny seed. Since it's anti-inflammatory and antioxidant, it's beneficial for preserving food. Cumin was a key ingredient for the ancient Egyptians when it came to the mummification process.

- **Mustard Seeds**

Mustard, a pungent spice, is great for fighting off unwanted bacteria that might ruin a meal. Historically, the waste of mustard seed was seen as low-value and disposed of as rapidly as possible. By using this waste, researchers believe that it might be beneficial in preserving food. In food preservation, mustard seeds' antibacterial qualities have been shown to be useful, and mustard seeds have been identified to assist in food preservation.

11.2 LIST OF RECOMMENDED FOODS

Do you currently have any of the goods listed below in your house? If not, I advise you to begin collecting them. These were all selected due to their large calorie content, strong nutritional value, and ease of long-term storage.

These cannot be purchased and then ignored. You should gather many more than you'll need, then consume them. Recycle your food stock. Replace the meal you just ate with something newer and fresher.

- **Rice**

Since the advent of agriculture, it has been essential to human agriculture and survival. Literally, all you need to make a high-calorie carbohydrate is water and heat. To look beautiful on the beach, we're not looking to lose all of our body fat and trim down to 5%. We can't afford to be very fussy about where we receive the energy we need.

- **Beans**

Your best options are black and pinto beans. Dry's take up less room and are simple to rehydrate overnight. They are calorie and protein dense and endure for a very long period.

- **Oils**

Ideally, avoid seed oils. Although seed oils are inexpensive, there is growing concern that they're not particularly healthy for you. Olive, coconut, and avocado oils are what you desire. They all keep up well, work well in the kitchen, and provide healthy fat for your diet. The greatest smoke point, or ability to resist burning, belongs to avocado. It is fantastic cooking oil, even if it lacks taste.

- **Lentils**

When properly cooked, foods high in protein store well and taste wonderful. A very undervalued food.

- **Nuts**

Extremely high in both fat and protein. They are perfect for on-the-go snacks since they don't need to be cooked or otherwise prepared, with the possible exception of seasoning with salt or other ingredients.

- **Animal fats**

Keep in mind that lipids are necessary to prevent hunger in rabbits. Keep all of the meat's fats. A cool, dry spot is the best way to keep anything that has cooked off. Just save the juice from a pound of bacon to fill a tiny mason jar. Hold onto your fats.

- **Vinegar**

Essential for making pickles. Many recipes call for it, including Chinese hot and sour soup. In addition, it functions as a cleaning agent without the toxins of many common chemicals. Similar to salt, this product is really cheap, so you may as well stock up. Baking is often seen as difficult and rewarding activity.

- **Canned Foods**

Particularly fruits and vegetables that have been preserved in cans. These are wholesome foods that, if improperly kept, won't keep very long. As we'll cover later in this chapter, you'll be producing the majority of these on your own.

- **Salt**

Essential for one's own well-being as well as for pickling. Additionally, most cuisine lacks flavor without it. Inexpensive and simple to locate.

- **Other Seasonings**

Contrary to popular belief, not everything has to be tasteless just because times are hard. Between the 12th and 18th centuries, Europe ruled the majority of the globe because they sought delicious cuisine. Have a lot of your preferred seasonings on hand. The majority have already been dried and are long-lasting, like everything you and your family like, including peppercorns, cumin, garlic powder, and cinnamon.

- **Vitamins**

Although it's preferable to get vitamins from food, if you're in a bind and can't acquire the

required nutrients elsewhere, certain tablets may assist in filling in the gaps. They may not be considered food, but they should still be mentioned.

11.3 FOOD PRESERVATIVES

According to the survival rule of threes, you may go up to three weeks in the wilderness without eating. Because of this, even though you may be famished when stranded in the wilderness, eating should be the very last thing on your mind.

Because it doesn't reach lethal levels until after three weeks of being stranded, your ability to acquire food is less concerning. But after all other necessities have been adequately taken care of, you may begin looking for food through foraging.

Not every seemingly edible food source you may encounter is safe to eat. The last thing you wish to do is ingest something that might be damaging to you since there are many dangerous and hazardous items out there. If you are unsure about something's identity while obtaining food to survive in the wilderness, especially when it comes to vegetation, don't eat it. Another general rule is to avoid anything bright in the wilderness. Fortunately, you have access to a wide variety of other dietary sources in the environment.

- **Garlic**

It is used by many preppers to frighten off insects. It is suitable for temporarily keeping goods. It has a bunch of dampness and infuses everything you store with scent.

- **Coal**

Used to remove moisture and smells.

- **Bay leaves**

They are used to scare off insects. Given that it is a dry substance, it is an excellent ally.

- **Satchels that absorb oxygen**

These sealed bags are used for packaging food with the intention of removing oxygen and extending the shelf life of the product. Bacteria and fungus cannot develop when oxygen is removed. These types of bags are used to store food using Mylar bags since they are used in restricted and completely sealed environments. Each packet includes iron powder (Fe) and other inert chemical substances. The iron in the bag reacts when it comes into touch with oxygen to form iron oxide. This reaction makes it possible to completely eliminate the oxygen. A well-executed technique may extend the food's shelf life to an average of 10 years.

Here are some suggestions for keeping certain foods:

- Lentils should be stored in a frigid, dry, and dark environment in an airtight container or sealed packaging. Because of their long shelf life, superior nutritional value, and capacity to thrive in drought-like circumstances, dried lentils are quite a common food in many countries. The preserved bean's color may somewhat deteriorate over time, but the taste will not change noticeably. Lentils that have come in contact with dampness or insects should be thrown away.

- Butter, seeds, and nuts must be stored in the freezer or refrigerator. They won't be bothered by the fluctuating kitchen temperatures and will be content and cold.

- All whole grains are stored in tight-fitting lidded or closed airtight containers. It's up to you what kind of container you want. Dry and sealed canisters and zip-lock bags of any material may serve their purpose as long as they are not porous.

- The berries should be evenly spread out and frozen until they are solid. In freezer bags, they may be stored for almost a year. To prevent freezer burn, be careful to remove as much air from the bags as you can.

- To quickly freeze vegetables, place them on a sheet pan with a rim. Once the frozen veggies have formed, store them in Ziplock bags or airtight containers. As much air as possible should be drawn out of the bags and filled to capacity with firm containers. Verify the dates on the packaging.

- Once opened, store maple syrup and honey in the refrigerator or in a cool, dark place. While creating the syrup, have fun with your family and remember to keep it correctly so that everyone may enjoy it on the pancake.

- The best place to store apple cider vinegar is in an airtight container in a cool, dark area out of direct sunlight, like a kitchen pantry or basement. Since refrigeration does not increase the shelf life of apple cider vinegar, it is not necessary.

- The majority of oils need to be stored in a cool environment, similar to a wine cellar. You should only purchase and store oil in dark glass containers that allow a small amount of light since light may rapidly harm an oil.

- Keeping eggs cool is the simplest way to preserve them. The natural coating on the outside of eggs keeps the egg within from degrading. In the event this is washed away, the eggs must be chilled.

- Yogurt should be kept in the refrigerator in its real, sealed container since it has a seven to fourteen-day shelf life. Spoon some of the cartons into a dish if it is not all eaten at once. Yogurt shouldn't be left out at ambient temperature for more than 2 hours.

- In general, the shelf life of low-acid canned items, including meat, fish, chicken, and the majority of vegetables, is two to five years. They must be stored in excellent condition and in a cool, dry place. You shouldn't utilize cans that are rusted, bulging, leaking, or otherwise damaged.

- Items that are properly sealed may be stored for a very long time. Although it is a common misconception, unsealed products should not be kept in their original packaging in the refrigerator because the iron and tin from the cans may mix into the food and impart a metallic taste. Repackaging leftovers in an airtight container and keeping them chilled can help you avoid this issue and keep them fresh.

- Jerky that has been properly dried lasts 2 weeks at ambient temperature in a sealed container. For best results, a longer shelf life, and the highest taste and quality, refrigerate or freeze the jerky.

- Make sure that the pan is securely covered and that the bars are stored in an airtight container in the refrigerator or freezer. Store the bars on a piece of butter paper between layers to prevent them from adhering to one another.

- Your stew, stock, or soup will keep in the fridge for three to four days. For easy reheating, single-serving portions should be kept in separate containers. For family meals, keep the soup in larger, airtight containers and take care to serve and reheat it according to temperature requirements.

- Milk containers should be covered and, if possible, kept away from items with strong aromas in the fridge because the milk may absorb these flavors. Milk should be chilled on the shelves of the refrigerator rather than on the warmer refrigerator doors.

- Once opened, oatmeal should be kept tightly packed in a Ziploc bag or a glass or plastic container. Oatmeal should ideally be consumed within a year after opening. In a freezer bag, dry oats can also be kept for up to a year. Your freezer must be kept at a constant 0 degrees Fahrenheit.

- Cooled dried fruits should be placed in small quantities in dried glass jars (preferably dark ones), cartons, freezer containers, or bags that are vapor and moisture-proof. When using glass containers, you may immediately observe the inside moisture buildup. Place the containers in a cool, dry, and well-lit area in the freezer or refrigerator.

- The easiest way to keep popped popcorn fresh is in an airtight container. Popcorn tins, as well as glass and plastic storage containers with sealable tops, are the best for preserving freshness. Look for freezer-safe containers if you wish to freeze the leftover popcorn.

- Pasta that is dry and uncooked may be kept for almost one year in a cool, dry place like your pantry. In order to keep its freshness, dry pasta has to be kept in an airtight box or container.

- Once opened, a peanut butter jar may stay in the refrigerator for at least three months. Without refrigeration, oil separation is possible.

- Chia seeds are to be kept in a plastic or glass container with a secure lid. Because of their antioxidants, chia seeds may be preserved for weeks in a dark, cool location, like your cupboard.

11.4 BOTULISM DISEASE

First and foremost, it must be made clear that botulism may poison you if you don't store wet and dry food properly in oxygen-reduced containers. This may occur with stored goods that are deemed to be wet. When attempting to consume them, you must be very careful and thorough. Check to see whether the food has been stored properly, how it was stored in the past, and if the bottle has holes, splits, or has changed shape or color. That is one approach to be sure that eating these foods won't result in botulism.

A bacterium called botulinum toxin, a neurotoxin, is what causes botulism, an illness that causes poisoning. You'll put out every effort to keep your family alive, but one mistake might cause them to get ill. Therefore, before eating the food, it is advised to boil it for 10 minutes after opening the containers. Any botulinum toxin which may have developed will be removed as a result.

Before placing things in the containers, we will use, we must first cook them in a pressure cooker. It is advised that these containers be made of glass and that they be vacuum sealed after being boiled with their appropriate lids. Aluminum bags with oxygen absorbers are another option. Here are a few of the symptoms brought on by the botulinum bacteria:

- Fatigue.
- Nausea.
- Vomiting.
- A dry mouth.
- Stomach aches.
- Breathing issues.
- No feeling in the body.
- Having trouble swallowing.
- Eyesight that is hazy or double.
- Weakening of the face on both sides.

Although this illness is infrequent, it is serious and has the potential to be lethal. We need containers to store them in order to create our food storage. We must remember that the intention is for it to continue for years if it is for a lengthy period. There will be goods that, with very good storage, can endure for between 20 and 30 years. According to research, if the packing technique is carried out correctly, they may live much longer.

11.5 TECHNIQUES FOR FOOD PRESERVATION

There are several things that could be beneficial at different points for people who live somewhat off the grid, whether they are city dwellers or homesteaders on a rural piece of land. Regardless of how far you've come from society or how distant you wish to go, you'll need food. People who desire to stay off the grid choose to cultivate or harvest their own vegetables, fruits, meat, and seeds, even if they live near a grocery shop. What should you do if you have too much of something and want it not to go to waste? For this reason, it is important to have a wide range of food preservation methods on hand. Preserving food requires a variety of methods, each with a varying shelf life and effectiveness depending on the food type. The date that your reserves were generated must be clearly marked on them as a result. If you lack motivation, these suggestions should help jumpstart your creative process.

11.5.1 FERMENTATION

Since the beginning of time, people have used fermentation as a safe method of food preservation. A month or more might pass when chopped vegetables are preserved in saline brine and kept in jars or ceramic crocks. Lower temperatures will extend the shelf life of jars. An added advantage of fermented foods is that they are a fantastic source of probiotics that will promote good healthy digestion and provide consumers' immune systems a much-needed boost. Almost any vegetable may be Lacto-fermented. Vegetables should be covered lightly with moderate salt brine and left to ferment at ambient temperature. Your beer will preserve its best texture and taste and postpone fermentation by cooling. Move the liquid to a cooler area when it starts to become foamy and smell somewhat sour. The easy process works because it generates an environment that is too acidic for the other bacteria to live. Lactobacilli bacteria that are present in almost all organic vegetables and fruits turn lactose into lactic acid. The saltwater brine aids in food preservation and adds to the sour flavor of fermented foods, along with the lactobacilli bacteria's ongoing development.

11.5.2 PICKLING

A traditional method of preserving a variety of foods, especially fruits and vegetables, is pickling. In the past, it was very difficult to preserve them for a longer length of time due to how fast they decay. Fruits and vegetables may be effectively preserved while maintaining their flavor and nutrients by pickling. The technique is effective because it stops germs from spreading within the food. The products are submerged in a solution that is heavily salted, spiced, sweetened, or acidified. The environment that results surrounding the meal is perfect for limiting bacteria development. The food is pickled in order to give it a rich, concentrated flavor while keeping it generally edible. Pickling is hence a method for food preservation when necessary.

11.5.3 FREEZING

It's a really simple procedure. Nearly everything can be frozen, but for certain items, a little advance preparation will make a difference in how well they turn out. It is a good idea to blanch most vegetables before freezing them. They will continue to taste and look fresher as a consequence. Most veggies may be blanched in 3 minutes of boiling, immediately followed by an ice bath. The majority of meats and fruits that are frozen may be eaten as is, but for extended storage, you might want to store the fruits in tiny portions on cookie trays first. Even a small chest freezer may have enough capacity to preserve a range of delicious meals, depending on your freezer space availability and your financial situation.

11.5.4 DEHYDRATION

This method is precisely the same as it seems it would be. If the food is dried and kept out of the environment, it will stop going bad. Because it's been preserved, it'll be able to be consumed for a much longer period. You can use a store-bought smoker if you don't have one, and if you do not wish to cook at home, you can utilize a dehydrator or a microwave in a low thermal setting. Various bananas, peppers, apples, berries, and other fruits and vegetables are very well suited for this process. Using this method, you may make jerky from whatever kind of beef cut you want, which will eventually allow you to utilize more of your food supply.

11.5.5 SMOKING

Another method to lose water is to smoke. Instead of utilizing an electrical dehydrator or similar heating equipment, dehydration is achieved via smoking. Because it dries out all the germs that dwell on the grains as well as removes moisture from them, it is perfect for dehydrating meat. Prior to the invention of electric smokers, the only method to smoke meat was over an open flame. Lighting the wood chip results in smoke, which gives the meat a robust flavor while gradually drying it.

11.5.6 SALTING

Meat may be preserved for a very long time without power via salt curing; in the past, communities and ship crews utilized this technique to preserve slain meat all year long. Today, it is still done. If you salt the meat, drain it, and hang it to mature for about 2 weeks, you may store it at ambient temperature for several months at a time. This stops the growth of germs. Dry-salting creates a hostile environment where no bacteria can survive, not even the salt-tolerant ones required for effective Lacto-fermentation. This process is also used while dry-curing capers and olives in addition to creating salted fish (bacalao). It also serves as the first step in various well-known meat preservation techniques, including smoking and freezing. In a jar, place the thing you want to preserve with salt on top of it. This is the simplest dry-salt remedy. The meal should then be re-layered, with a fresh layer going on top after another salting of the dish's surface. Continue in this manner until the meal has been consumed in its entirety or the container is full. The final step is to sprinkle salt over the surface. Before utilizing your dry-salted food, you should soak it for a day to eliminate the bulk of the salt; often, change the water throughout this process.

11.6 PACKAGING TECHNIQUES

Utilizing techniques that enhance the quality and integrity of the seeds, especially white rice seeds, is crucial when storing seeds. The fact is that an insect known as the "weasel" deposits its eggs inside the plants, especially in ripe plants. They may contain their larvae for years and reactivate at any time. While the grain is being stored, this larva may escape. The following technique is time-consuming yet effective. Place the whole seed package in the freezer for two days. After that, let it out for a day before re-freezing it for two further days. Take the seeds out of the original bag as soon as you take them out of the freezer and let them air dry before storing them. You will have eliminated any larvae or insects that were within the seeds using this technique.

Depending on where you want to store the food, there are several packaging techniques. I have many labeled containers. Let's now examine the food's storage practices extending its shelf life.

You'll need the following implementations:

a) Pen

b) Bucket

c) Alcohol

d) Matches

e) Pet container

f) Laurels with dried leaves

g) A medium-thick transparent plastic square.

h) A kitchen plate made of paper that is about 1.5 cm square.

i) Cotton is a little ball that can fit through the bottle's spout.

j) Bottle cap a black bag covering the whole bottle (optional) notebook.

k) Plastic bags (polyethylene terephthalate, or pet in boat).

l) Heat sealer, a clothes iron (which you use with a bucket and wood), or hair iron scissors.

m) Metal or plastic funnel. If you don't have one, you may make one by removing the bottle's spout.

n) Charcoal that has been well cleaned and dried in little pieces (absorbs smells and moisturizes).

- **O_2 sachet in PET bottle**

The best thing to do if any of the oxygen-absorbing supplies you purchase are packaged together in the same bag is to store them in another sealed plastic bag until you need them. In this manner, they will come into touch with oxygen as little as possible.

This is due to the fact that you only have five minutes to handle the explosives outside since they are activated by contact with the oxygen in the environment.

Another method of preserving food in PET bottles is to use oxygen-absorbing bags. Well, this technique entails pouring the wine into the bottle and positioning the bay leaves, similar to the previous method. Following that, you must add an oxygen-absorbing sachet to the bottle containing the remedy.

Quickly close it and line the lid with grey adhesive tape. Another sealing technique is to coat the lid with melted paraffin. Wait until the next day to ensure the technique was applied correctly.

- **O$_2$ sachet in Mylar bag**

Tiny quantities are stored using this method, and only small bags are utilized. Examples include dehydrated food, fragrant herbs, salt, sugar, chocolate, etc. With the oxygen absorption socks, I also advise utilizing Mylar bags for critical documents that you wish to keep. In reality, you may use them for anything with 10% or less humidity.

It is crucial to seal the Mylar bags by using a hair iron or iron to remove as much air as possible. You should do a heat test beforehand to prevent incidents that might cause the content to be spoiled.

- **O$_2$ sachet in Mylar bag and airtight bucket**

If you're going to use Mylar bags, you must remove any jewelry from your fingers and wrists, including watches and other accessories, since you might damage them without realizing it. Try to simply use your fists to press the food down when you open the Mylar bag and place it inside. This is done to compress it so tightly that there are no air spaces. Keep your hands shut, and refrain from using your fingers.

Continuing, I'll now demonstrate two variations of this technique for you:

1. **<u>Keep a single food item in an airtight bucket in a large Mylar bag</u>**

The chosen food must be completely filled into the bag. Little by little, using your knuckles, arrange the food until there is just 4 cm left before you reach the bag's edge. You should wipe the inside of the Mylar bag's edge with a clean, dry cloth before you begin sealing. When using any storage technique with this kind of bag, you must do this since the food may release some dust and prevent you from sealing the bag properly. To make the seal, you must leave at least 5 to 6 cm of the Mylar bag free. There are many methods to do this, but one of the simplest is to leave space in the upper half of the bag for the oxygen absorbent sack. This should be in the center of the inside side of the bag so that it can absorb the oxygen evenly when the Sacket enters and falls into the middle of the Mylar bag. When everything is organized and the sealer is nearby

(a hair iron or clothes iron with the proper temperature), swiftly fold the bag, sucking out as much air as you can, and seal the opening you left to place the wallet inside the bag.

This should only take you five minutes to complete.

Otherwise, the oxygen-absorbent sachet will stop working and won't be able to remove the air from the bag since it will activate when you take it out. As a result, it is recommended that you keep them tightly closed and that you immediately close the bag in which you keep them after removing a set from where they are stored.

This method extends the shelf life of food and protects it against moisture, insects, and rodents.

2. **Food servings are packaged in paper bags, oxygen-absorbing sachets, and Mylar bags, and all of them are contained within an airtight bucket**

Before using this technique to store food, you must remove all the packaging that was included when you purchased the food, divide it out, and place it exclusively in paper bags (for example, craft). The bag should then be adhered to using paper tape (masking tape), and this should be tightly fastened since there must be any loose spaces. Additionally, each bag must have the storage date written on it. You must do this because if the absorbers weren't in the paper bags, they wouldn't be able to remove the oxygen.

Example: (You already have the refrigeration technique to eliminate any vermin.) White rice. Fill a paper bag with the recipe to provide my family with enough food for a week. Then, wrap the bag and affix masking tape (paper tape) to it, along with the contents and the date of storage. Do the same with the items you can consume in a month, including salt, sugar, spices, beans, oatmeal, and other foods. To prevent air bubbles, everything is placed inside the Mylar bags in their respective paper bags. Everything must fit snugly up until about 3 cm before the edge of the bucket, at which point we must seal it off, leaving space for an oxygen-absorbent sac according to the bag's capacity or size. If it is large, you can fold it, store it inside, and use it again later without having to cut it. If you choose to open the bag, you can do so by cutting the seal and resealing it with another oxygen-absorbing sac.

Utilizing a vacuum cleaner is another method for sealing. Utilize the smaller needle and place it inside the Mylar bag.

You'll see that the bottle has deformed and hardened because the sachet has completely absorbed the oxygen.

11.7 CONTAINER LABELING

You'll need to identify the containers in which you want to store your food, and in order to do so, you will need:

- A pen
- Paper bags
- Persistent markers
- Stacks of paper
- A small-sized notebook
- Use only on plastics intended for outdoor use, scotch, or plastic tape.
- Masking tape is only to be used outside of mylar or aluminum storage bags.

You must record the day on which you are packing it, the kind of food, the amount, the product's expiration date, etc. This history belongs to you and your family. Note what you believe is necessary for your family in writing.

11.8 WATER STORAGE

The water supply is always reliable. In the event that you keep it at home under your supervision, there are techniques to recover it. Algae or pathogens may eventually develop in the water if the container is not cleaned properly or if it has been sitting around for a long time. The best method of recovery is to boil it for a few minutes or add a few drops of chlorine (bleach) to the water and leave it outside for a few hours to make the smell and taste go away.

If the water appears cloudy and smells bad, it is preferable to add twice as much chlorine, air it by moving it from one vessel to another and leave it for several hours. If possible, it is preferable to have a filter that you can make at home and use to clean the water of impurities in addition to the chlorine.

Needed for only one person (minimum):

- To cook with (12 liters).
- Personal hygiene half a liter.
- 2 liters (or half a gallon) of water per person each day.

Example:

(4 drops of chlorine added to 2 liters of water)

(4 drops of chlorination added to 12 gallons of water)

Other water-purifying liquids and tablets exist, although their availability varies by country. You should check for more information in your region.

- **HDPE 2 water containers**

These are available in various sizes. They are unique water containers. Whether they have a pipe or not really depends on your taste. These containers are often blue in color. You should search for them in your city's stores.

There are also emergency containers that look like really large bags that you may place in the tubs and fill with water. You may search the internet for a wide variety of water containers and pick the best alternative for where you live.

If you want to collect water from nature, you might consider methods like rainwater collection, fogging, natural water wells, etc., by analyzing the climate of your region. You will need several techniques for treating the water, which you must research online and implement.

Chapter 12:

THE ULTIMATE COOKBOOK FOR PREPPERS

It's easy to misunderstand what goes into a dish. It's possible for anybody to successfully follow a recipe with a little forethought and planning beforehand. However, the true test of a great chef is whether they can follow a recipe step-by-step. A perfectly planned meal might go awry for a variety of reasons, including a lack of certain foods, a lack of certain equipment, the special dietary needs of the person you're serving, or any of the many other possibilities. A well-prepared individual should have all of these ingredients and equipment on hand while preparing these meals, which is why they are among my favorites. Preparation, on the other hand, assumes that something will go wrong. Because you'll have to adapt to a circumstance when the recipe isn't ideal, now is the best moment to learn how to cook.

12.1 Foods you can make without appliances

None of them need electricity or specialized equipment to complete. Instead, these are easy to prepare using a fire, a knife, a saucepan, and a stick.

12.1.1 Rabbit stew

- ➢ **Preparation time: 10 minutes**
- ➢ **Cooking time: 2 hours**
- ➢ **Servings: 6-8**

<u>Ingredients:</u>

- 2 pounds of rabbit meat, cut into (2-inch) pieces (sprinkle with ¼ teaspoon black pepper and 1 teaspoon of salt)
- 4 bacon strips
- 2 onions, chopped
- 1 can of beer (optional)
- 3 carrots, chopped
- ¼ cup tomato paste

- 1 teaspoon garlic

- 2 ribs celery, chopped

- 1 teaspoon sugar

- 2 ½ cups of chicken stock

- Salt and ground black pepper to taste

Directions:

1. Put everything in a saucepan. Bring to a boil by heating.

2. Include the lid. 2 hours of covered simmering, or until the stew is fork-tender. Delicious with mashed potatoes.

Nutritional facts: Calories:

340; Fat: 20g; Carb: 16g; Protein: 24g

12.1.2 LENTIL LEBANESE SOUP

- ➢ **Preparation time: 10 minutes**
- ➢ **Cooking time: 45 minutes**
- ➢ **Servings: 4**

Ingredients:

- 6 cups of chicken/beef stock

- 3 tablespoons olive oil

- 1 (large) yellow onion, chopped

- 1 tablespoon garlic, minced

- 1 pound of red lentils

- 1 tablespoon cumin, ground

- 1 or 2 lemons, juice

- ½ teaspoon cayenne

- Salt and pepper to taste

- ½ cup cilantro, chopped

- 2 celery stalks, diced

- 1 bunch of collards, kale, or chard

- 2 carrots, diced

Directions:

1. In a saucepan, combine the water, lentils, and broth. Once it begins to boil, turn down the heat, cover the pan with a top, and allow the mixture to simmer for 25 to 30 minutes.

2. When the veggies are added, replace the lid, and cook them for a further 15 to 20 minutes, or until they are soft. The aromatics—cilantro, garlic, and lemon—should be added last. After that, give it only two more minutes.

3. Get rid of the heat. Add any leafy greens you want to use right away. For another 8 to 10 minutes or so, cover and let go. If you have surpluses from this recipe, be sure to refrigerate them or can them.

Nutritional facts: Calories:

271; Fat: 8g; Carb: 43g; Protein: 9g

12.1.3 Rice and Red Beans

➤ **Preparation time: 15 minutes**

➤ **Cooking time: 2 hours**

➤ **Servings: 4-6**

Ingredients:

- 1 cup onion, diced
- 4 cups of broth or more
- 3/4 cup green peppers, finely diced
- 1 turkey, smoked
- 3/4 cup celery, finely diced
- ½ teaspoon of cayenne pepper
- 1 teaspoon thyme, dried
- 1 pound of (red) kidney beans
- 12 ounces of andouille sausage, cubed
- 4 cloves minced garlic
- 2 bay leaves
- Black pepper, to taste
- Rice

Directions:

1. Put the dried beans in a basin with water, cover it, and let them soak all night if necessary.

Use lots of water because these items will swell to up to twice their original size.

2. When it's time to cook, heat up a pot, add some oil, and add the meat. Add the vegetables once they are 70% cooked. Add the seasoning once those appear soft.

3. Add the drained red beans. The water that remains after rehydrating them is not what you want. Put the broth in. If 4 cups are insufficient, add more until everything is covered. Turn up the heat until it begins to boil. The lid is on and reduces the heat to medium-low for around an hour.

4. Check on it an hour later. The beans can start to be mashed if they are soft. Some people prefer it mashed more than others. Everything depends on you. Squeezing them with a spoon against the edge of the saucepan will do the trick. This is a fun task for kids, so consider using them if you have some on hand. If it seems to be cooking down too much, add extra broth.

5. Now would be a perfect time to prepare the rice since those beans will cook for a further 30 minutes.

6. Use only a saucepan with a tightly fitting cover. Rice cookers are used by all technologically savvy individuals since rice is very difficult to prepare and requires experience to perfect. Rice and water should be added to a saucepan in a 1:2 ratio. A little bit is often enough. 2 cups of water and one cup of rice should be plenty. Add a few sprinkles of salt and some oil. Lard or butter are excellent alternatives.

7. Rice and water should be heated to a boil over high heat. Reduce the temperature to the absolute minimum right away, then top it with a cover. NEVER TAKE OFF THE LID. You'll muck it up. Give it 15 to 20 minutes to gently cook and soak in the water. Now let some steam out by removing the lid for only 2 seconds. Place the lid back on and leave it without heat for a further 10 minutes.

8. Remove the cover and give it a fork flush after 10 minutes have passed.

9. Rice and beans should be served together. Beans and rice are among the ideal meals for surviving or otherwise since they are very affordable, tasty, and full.

Nutritional facts: Calories:

335; Fat: 1g; Carb: 68g; Protein: 14g

12.1.4 TRAIL MIX

> ➤ **Preparation time: 5 minutes**
> ➤ **Cooking time: 0 minutes**
> ➤ **Servings: 4-5 cups**

Ingredients:

- ½ cup pumpkin seeds, raw
- 3/4 cup cashews, raw
- ½ cup sunflower seeds, raw
- ½ cup (unsulfured, unsweetened) raisins
- 3/4 cup pecans, raw
- ¼ teaspoon sea salt
- ½ cup (unsulfured, unsweetened) cherries
- ½ cup (82% dark) chocolate, chopped
- ½ teaspoon cinnamon
- A pinch of nutmeg

Directions:

1. Similar to combining ingredients in a bag. Your favorite dried fruit, nuts, and other treats should be combined.
2. Make sure to cut them very finely. Put salt in. A fantastic small snack for when you're taking a break and last in the field.

Nutritional facts: Calories:

237; Fat: 14g; Carb: 24g; Protein: 6g

12.1.5 FISH TACOS

> ➢ **Preparation time: 10 minutes**
> ➢ **Cooking time: 30 minutes**
> ➢ **Servings: 4**

Ingredients:

- 2 tablespoons of oil
- Fish, cleaned
- Salt and pepper to taste

Directions:

1. For a variety of tacos, you may create your own tortillas using maize from your yard.
2. Cook until the fish is ready to eat. Oil should be added to a skillet. The corn tortilla should have some water applied on both sides. If you don't do that, the tortilla will end up being dry and crumbly, and it will easily catch on fire. It becomes pliable and steams when some water is added. Heat until only several brown spots start to emerge on each side. Before it becomes cold, serve immediately.
3. Salt and pepper on fish are excellent. If you've previously caught and cleaned one in a local river, this shouldn't be an issue.

Nutritional facts:

Calories: 214; Fat: 14g; Carb: 28g; Protein: 20g

CONCLUSION

Since the planet's first signs of life, an uninterrupted line of survivors has been responsible for raising each of us. Everybody has the ability to carry on that legacy. Humans are among the most resilient species; that is why we can survive on seven continents, including the Mediterranean's marvelous Eden-like surroundings, the deserts' sweltering heat and dryness, the tundra's freezing temperatures, the jungles' diseases and carnivores, and the mountains' low oxygen and perilous topography. Preparation doesn't take much time. It doesn't call for a significant change in politics, beliefs, or way of life. In order to become someone who can get themselves — and the people they care about — through the hardships that countless individuals went through before us, all it takes is a little bit of education, effort, and consciousness. There is a method that the world should operate. Even if we frequently disagree on the specifics, we all have a general idea of what it looks like. But knowing what they should and shouldn't be and how they aren't always similar is a part of growing up. Every parent has at least once remarked to their child, and from the youngster's point of view, it's among the most upsetting things they've ever heard, "Life isn't fair". That sentence appears harsh just from hearing it. But that also often turns out to be the case. Take this advice from your parents and behave as a result.

Instead of waiting for assistance, provide it. Be the one that other people hope would rescue them, not the one who prays to be saved. Because they are the finest justification for existing at all, look out for yourself and the ones who mean to you the most. Be careful while you're outside.

Being prepared is a wise move. It's not only about being ready for the worst; it's also about being ready to live and thrive in every circumstance that comes your way. You will learn how to be self-sufficient and survive on your own resources from this book, even if society as we know it collapses around us. This book is not just useful for preppers and survivalists but for everyone. This guide includes something for everyone, whether you want to learn more about prepping or are just preparing yourself for everyday emergencies.